LISTEN

PETER SZENDY

A HISTORY OF OUR EARS

LISTEN

Preceded by *Ascoltando* by Jean-Luc Nancy

Translated by Charlotte Mandell

FORDHAM UNIVERSITY PRESS)) NEW YORK)) 2008

Library of Congress Cataloging-in-Publication Data
Szendy, Peter.
[Écoute. English]
Listen : a history of our ears / Peter Szendy ; preceded by Ascoltando / by Jean-Luc Nancy ; translated by Charlotte Mandell.
    p.   cm.
Includes bibliographical references (p.   ) and index.
ISBN 978-0-8232-2799-0 (cloth : alk. paper)—
ISBN 978-0-8232-2800-3 (pbk. : alk. paper)
1. Music—Philosophy and aesthetics.   2. Music—History and criticism.
3. Musical criticism.   I. Nancy, Jean-Luc.   II. Title.
ML3800.S9613   2007
781.1′7—dc22

                                                                    2007046205

Printed in the United States of America
10 09 08   5 4 3 2 1

Originally published as *Ecoute: une histoire de nos oreilles* (Paris: Editions de Minuit, 2001).

TO JULIE L.

CONTENTS

Following the example of composers, who were never shy of in-
venting terms for tempos, and on the model of *cantando* or
scherzando, reading Peter Szendy makes me think of the marking
ascoltando: "listening."[1] It directs us to play while listening: while
listening to what?—What else but the music that one is playing?

It is immediately obvious that this marking could not have
any specificity, since no instrumentalist plays any other way but
while listening. What is playing, if not listening right through
from beginning to end: to hear the score that is written so as to
understand it, to examine it or *auscultate* it, taste it, then while
playing it not to stop listening and experiencing the music that
resounds—one could say *sentire* or feel it, still in Italian where
the general term for sensibility or sensoriality also designates listening (so the tempo marking could also be *sentendo*).[2]

Ascoltando is the secret direction for every musical performance. In music it designates an element in music that is never
lacking in any phenomenon of sensibility, hence one that is not
absent from any of the other arts, but that is brought out in all its
fullness in music: it is the element of a formative repeat [*renvoi
constitutive*], a resonance or a reverberation, a return to itself by
which alone the "self" in question can take place. To feel is always also to feel oneself feel [*se sentir sentir*], but the subject who
feels "himself" thus does not exist or is "himself" only in this

feeling, through it and even actually as it. There is no subject that is not a sentient subject. No feeling—no sensation, emotion, or sense in any sense of the word—that does not on its own form the recursion or loop by which a subject takes place. "Self" is never anything but *to* self, *in* self or *for* self: it is never anything but a return, a reminder, a relationship, a transfer, and at the bottom of all this reversion an original, generative repetition, by which the *to self* occurs.

Sonority forms more than one privileged model for this return [*renvoi*] that precedes and forms every statement [*envoi*] of a theme, a *sensing* [sentant] in general. Sonority essentially *re-sounds*: it is in itself resonance. One could say that the echo is part of the sound, that it belongs to its immanence—but that reflection is not in the same way part of form or of visible color. Reflection requires a reflective surface, in principle external to the visible thing. Resonance is inside of sound itself: a sound is its own echo chamber, just as it is its own timbre, its overtones, and what is called its color.[3] The ancient Greek *êkhéô*, from which "echo" comes, means "to make noise" as well as "to re-sound": it signifies precisely "to return a sound." A sound is always "returned," restored: it is restored from itself to itself. A sonorous body that is struck *returns* the blow by the sound that is the vibration of the blow itself. Sound is at the same time *struck* (pinched, rubbed, breathed, etc.), *returned*, and *heard* [entendu, understood] in the precise sense that it *is understood* [s'entend] or that it *makes itself heard* [se fait entendre]: and for that, in that, it *listens to itself* [s'écoute].

But what is a subject that is thus constituted in listening, or as a subject that is *ascoltando*? It is no more the individual interpreting the work than the one who composed it or the one who listens to it: it is not even the union of these three people into one single entity, as very commonly happens when a composer plays his own music. The subject who is constituted in resonance, the listening-subject, is nothing else, or is no one else, but the music itself, more precisely nothing else but the musical work.[4] The work is what refers [*renvoie*] to itself, and in a certain way the entire work [*ouvrage*] of this work [*oeuvre*] consists in this referral, by which alone it is possible—and necessary—for the work to refer and send itself [*renvoie et s'envoie*] to the outside (to the world, to the soul). Thus "listening is immanent to the work: it is an activity of the musical subject."[5]

When Peter Szendy summons as he does, in a truly unprecedented and *unheard of* [inouïe] way, all these examples or aspects of listening and hearing that include arrangement, plagiarism, quotation, variation, or reinstrumentation, but also the public concert, its stage and its echoes (the applause), as well as the "diseased auditory nerves" of Beethoven, then the proliferating register of all the instrumentations of modern listening that are at the same time conditions for reproduction, distribution, and resonance of music, and that can also become its conditions of production (DJ, mix)—when he makes us lend an ear to our ears, which we thought we would never hear, his work of virtuoso performance in fact allows us to perceive an ample gearing down of the most original, most structural, and most dynamic reality—the most secret, too—of music. The figures of the listener, the arranger, the record, the headphones, are so many expansions or fragmentations of the single musical referral [*renvoi*]—unique in its duplication, in its covering distance, and in its *resounding* within a perceptible space that it opens and that must always in fact, in principle, have the form or ideality of an ear and its pinna.

Pavillon, pinna: the meaning of this word in acoustics was formed by analogy with the form of a tent in the shape of a pavilion—and this first meaning was connected with the wings of the butterfly [*papillon*]. There is the bell [*pavillon*] of a trumpet and that of the ear: one opening onto the other, the other resonating from the one. The one in the other, in short, and the one through the other: two solid embouchures, in contact with each other to form *what listens to itself*, that is to say a musical subject—and with it, something that could indeed turn out in the end to constitute nothing less than *the subject of a subject* in general.

By "subject of a subject," I mean to convey both the pitch of a subjectivity or a "subjectity" [*subjectité*]: the infinite vanishing point of return to self, of folding-over or folding-back in which the "self" consists (and thus does not consist, but resounds and distances itself in itself from itself)—and the *theme* of the subject, a theme that is asymptotically confused with its tonality as well as with its movement or tempo: this would be the theme and tempo, precisely, of the infinite distancing of proximity to self, of Augustine's *interior intimo meo et superior summo meo* by which the form of the subject that has left its mark on history until the present day is straightaway presented. "The subject of a subject" is also, thus, a rhythm, a reprise, a reduction of its theme and its hearings: always more than a listening, as well as always more than a performance, more than an interpretation. The score doesn't stop being shared.

What listens to itself [*s'écoute*], in this sense, is not what remains near one and what is heard silently in its own immediacy.[6] What listens to itself, no doubt, can come dangerously close to narcissism[7] (but is there a way, when in the vicinity of the subject, simply to have done with narcissism? And how, and where, can one locate the difference, which is in fact visible and audible, between Echo and Narcissus?). Still, what listens to itself is not just what resounds in the self and what rebounds to the self: this same movement, and this very movement, places it outside of self and makes its rebound overflow. Basic repetition—the repetition *of the basis* and *as basis*—is also, by itself, an excess, a carrying away. Music places us outside of ourselves: our whole tradition has known this, and it is with a penetration of the greatest rigor that Nietzsche could outline, facing what he called "metaphysics," the improbable image of a "musician Socrates." This Socrates cannot himself be heard without immediately being scattered into as many hearings as listeners whom he opens with his tongue, whose ears he forces open with his vibrant wasp- or torpedo-tongue.

In many respects, music is probably the practice of art that has for a century experienced the most considerable technical transformations—both from the point of view of its procedures and its internal materials (the ensemble of its sonorous values), and from the point of view of its methods of reproduction, am- plification, propagation, which have also become, through elec- tronics, methods of creation for which the name "synthesizer" could constitute a kind of symbol.[8] At the same time, and conse- quently (if at least one can simply disentangle here the causes from the consequences . . .), the ensemble of social or cultural conditions of musicality have been profoundly changed. It is probably not by chance that, from the successive moments of jazz, country, and rock, a worldwide musical space has also been greatly reshaped, or even completely created, opening in its turn possibilities seized through rhythms, timbres, and structures found in lost traditions or in invented instrumentations. More and more, one is tempted to say, music is listening to itself: it openly presents itself as this subject-work (even if it is pure im- provisation) that is linked to nothing so much as to itself,[9] to the proximity *and* to the strangeness of its own resonance, even more than to some finality or content, whether it is in the order of forms of composition or in that of significations. It is the proximity of our strangeness that is inflected: the approach of our distancing, which gives today its unsettling and yet urgent figure to what we no longer know well how to call "a future" [*un avenir*].

Why did Nietzsche speak about the "music of the future"? Is the future [*l'avenir*], or the yet-to-come [*l'à venir*], always above all musical?

LISTEN

—where "I'm listening" also means "listen to me"

I forget when I listened to music for the first time. Maybe some people remember the unique, singular impression that launched their history of listening. Not me. It seems to me there has always been music around me; impossible to say if—and when—it began one day.

Even more improbable, undiscoverable, as if it were drowned in the flood of shapeless memories, is the moment when I began to *listen to music as music.* With the keen awareness that it was *to be understood* [entendre], deciphered, pierced rather than perceived. If this moment, like the other, can't be situated in my immemorial past, what I know or think I know, on the other hand, is that musical listening that is *aware of itself* has always been accompanied in me with the feeling of a *duty.* Of an imperative: you *have* to listen, one *must* listen. It seems to me that my activity as a conscious listener, knowingly listening to music *for the music,* has never existed without a feeling of *responsibility,* which may perhaps have preceded the *right* that was given me to lend an ear.

You have to listen! If the injunction, in this imperative, does not brook any question (*you have to!*), the activity it prescribes (*listen*) seems to me less and less defined: What is listening, what is the listening that responds to a *you must*? Is it even an activity? By thinking that I am *doing* something by listening (that I am doing something to the work or the author, for example), aren't I already in the process of betraying the injunction itself, the *you must* that orders me to be *all hearing*, to do nothing in order only to listen?

There is a memory, perhaps a little late, but one that today seems just as closely linked to *each* of my listenings as that archaic *you must*: it is that of listening to music with the idea of sharing this listening—my own—of addressing it to another person. I remember, for instance, the fascinating hearing of the slow movement—"nocturne"—of the *Music for Strings, Percussion, and Celesta* by Bartók, in my uncle's room, in Budapest. We were both listening to it, in silence, scarcely disturbed but rather confirmed in our listening by the crickets in the garden, at night. We were listening to a version I have forgotten, which figured in a compilation entitled *Do You Like Bartók? (Szereti ön Bartókot?)*. An intense listening, indeed, full of adventures, strange events, dreams . . . but that did not come to itself until after the fact, when we decided to address it to someone else. This was my cousin: with her child's ears (she was five years old and I was eight) she heard with terror something that, in the opening bars, must have seemed like a contraption of fabulous insects.

So it was in those moments that, not without some perversion, my uncle and I took pleasure in the terrifying power of this music over a child; it was in these moments that, addressed to another, our listening truly became *ours*: a sign of complicity, a work of collaboration.

Later on, and more simply, I wanted to share my listenings; I enjoyed doing so. As if I wanted to affix a lasting mark on them that would show they were mine and would make them, if not perennial, at least *transmissible* to others.

It's true: each time I want to *sign my listening*. Not with the authority of the music critic or musicologist who would say: such-and-such version of such-and-such work is better than any other, such-and-such pianist played the Sonata Opus *X* tonight better than he ever played it before, by respecting its architecture, structure, details, phrasing, and so on. No, it is more simply *as a listener* that I want to sign my listening: I would like to point out, to identify, and to share such-and-such sonorous event that *no one besides me*, I am certain of it, has ever heard as I have. There is no doubt about that. And I am even convinced that musical listening exists only insofar as this desire and conviction exist; in other words, that listening—and not hearing or perception—begins with this legitimate desire to be signed and addressed. To others.

Except: How can a listening become *my own*, identifiable as *my own*, while still continuing to answer to the unconditional injunction of a *you must*? What space of appropriation does music reserve for its listeners so that they can in turn sign the listening of a work, an interpretation, an improvisation (in order to address it, to share it as *their own*)?

As a listener, I sometimes have the impression of having been in every music profession, occupied all the positions: by turns composer (of small forgotten masterpieces, ones that are simply imagined, glimpsed), editor, copyist (when I send you, on a little staff scribbled on a postcard, a theme I love so), improviser for a moment (when I try to add a few piano concertante notes to the orchestra of Bach's Brandenburg Concertos, like a somewhat sacrilegious karaoke performer), even conductor (beating out the measure and signaling the entries, implacably marking the nuances of some favorite in my music collection) . . .

Now, all these professions have their rights, responsibilities, duties. Explicit and clearly codified, after a long judicial history, fascinating and conflicted. But what about me? Me as a listener? Does my *you must*, this injunction that accompanies me, have anything to do with the prescriptions that rule said musical professions?

As a listener, so often occupying or usurping all roles, it seems that I have no duty, no responsibility, no account to make to anyone. Flighty and fickle or attentive and concentrating, silent or dissolute, is listening strictly my private affair? But then, from where does this *you must*, which dictates my duties, come to me? And what are these duties? This *you must* that always accompanies me, that sends this demand to me: to whom am I accountable, to whom and to what do I have to answer?

There is, to my knowledge, no explicit mention, in the entire history of texts forming the corpus of what we call author's rights [*droit d'auteur*] or copyright, of any sort of *listener's rights* [droit de l'auditeur]. Nothing about what he has a right to expect, nor his possible responsibilities, nor his duties. And yet, in this vast field of history of law in music, which is still largely unexplored, I look unceasingly. For what, exactly? Probably for the *implicit* outlines of what *could* be my right, my jurisprudence, my legislation. As a listener.

My explicit obligations (for I exaggerate, there are a few) can be counted on the fingers of one hand: keep silent during classical concerts (an obligation often printed on the back of programs);[1] pay for my seat; pay tax on copies and recordings for private use (it is included in the price of new tapes or compact discs) and do not use them for public purposes or commercial distribution; finally, sometimes but not always, keep the noise level below a nighttime or daytime racket. That's about it, I don't think I've left anything else out.

Of course, this *you must* that has always accompanied me is not reduced, far from it, to these few objective external constraints, even if it is still not independent of them. But I am just as convinced that this *you must* is not purely internal either, subjective, singular. It has a history: a history that is not only *my* history.

That is why I look desperately, in the forensic history of music, for any place where there is a question of me, the listener. I know in advance that this quest is doomed to failure. But I'll go look anyway: for my rights and my duties, since they have never been explicitly codified, stem implicitly from laws that, little by little, have ended up ruling musical life: authors, adaptors, arrangers, publishers, record producers, interpreters . . . I can, up to a certain point, find myself in them, investigate the objective history of their *you must* to reflect on my own and put it in perspective. And moreover, it goes without saying, their disagreements— especially those innumerable and fascinating trials that we can find in archives and transcripts—have so often been pleaded, regulated, negotiated *for me*: taking me, the listener, as a witness or pretext for their conflicting interests.

Who has a right to music? Who can hear it as if it belonged to him, who can appropriate it? Who has the right to make it *his own?*

Every listener asks these questions, whether he is aware of it or not, whether he wants to or not. I ask these questions as soon as I want to make you hear *this*: some bars from *Don Giovanni*, some of Glenn Gould's breathing, some murmuring in an improvisation by Keith Jarrett, some accent or silence in Bill Evans, some throbbing in the *Sacre du Printemps*, what else . . . In short, a "beautiful passage," a *favorite moment* in my own musical library. Simply to prepare you to hear these moments *as I hear them*, I begin to describe them to you—but barely—with words. And immediately I begin to lose them. When we listen, both of us, and when I sense, as if by telepathy, that what you are listening to is so far from what I would have liked to make you hear, I tell myself: this moment might not have been my own, after all. For what I wanted to hear you listening to—yes: *to hear you listening to!*—was *my listening*. Perhaps an impossible wish—the impossible itself.

Despite my vexation (it is always immense), I wonder: Can one *make a listening listened to?* Can I transmit *my* listening, unique as it is? That seems so improbable, and yet so desirable, so necessary too. For I imagine that this irrepressible desire is not only my desire as a simple listener: I imagine that a pianist, a composer, in short a musician who, unlike me, is not content with playing words or his record player also wishes, above all else, to make a listening listened to. *His* listening.

What can I do, then, to make this listening listened to, my own? I can repeat, I can replay a few measures over and over, and I can say and say again what I hear. Sometimes I manage it. Sometimes you listen to me listening. I hear you listen to me listening. But it's so rare.

If I were a musician, more a musician than a simple listener or player of record players and words, I would probably begin to rewrite. To adapt, to arrange. I would emphasize a phrase, I would repeat a note, I would shorten a measure to highlight a theme, I would imagine and perhaps transcribe the virtual orchestra that I hear so that it plays to you, under my direction, the exact inflection of this moment, duly prepared and artfully abandoned, as it resounds *exactly* to my ear. I would make myself into an adaptor, transcriber, orchestrator—in short an *arranger* to sign and cosign *my* listening in the work of another.

There in fact exist, in the history of music, listeners who have *written down their listening*. These are so-called arrangers, who have fascinated me for a long time, such a long time.

A theme of so-and-so arranged in the style of someone else, Ellington in Monk, Bach in Webern, Beethoven in Wagner . . . The arranger (who can moreover be an author now and again) is not merely a virtuoso of styles: he is a musician who knows how to *write down a listening*; who knows how, with any sonorous work, to *make it listened to as* . . . It's a little like my uncle and me, with the addition of writing and art. It's a little as if my uncle and I had decided to make our listening *recognized*, not to save it for one single person, for a child; as if we had wanted to address our listening to a real *public*. And it is from this *public* quality of the arrangement that all the legal questions follow: namely, the necessity of obtaining the author's agreement, faithfulness or unfaithfulness to the original, possible accusations of plagiarism or pastiche, in short, the *right*, this time explicit and vigilant, that traces the outlines and legitimate frontiers of the *adaptation of a work.*

Let us suppose, then, that, like Liszt transcribing Beethoven, like Schoenberg orchestrating Bach, like Gould adapting Wagner for the piano, I manage to make you listen to my listening. Do I have the *right* to do that? Do they have, did they have the *right*? And if yes, what, beyond the simple desire or pleasure of someone or other (my own, their own), *justifies* such a transcription? Isn't that the worst of betrayals of what, precisely, one should have wanted to make heard? Can one only make one's listening heard by rewriting, by radically crossing out the work to be heard? Can one adapt, transcribe, orchestrate, in short arrange *in the name of the work?* In the name of a listening *to the work?*

These are the most pressing, most urgent questions in this book.

Who has a right to music? Who can make it heard as he hears it?

These questions have often given rise to *sociological* answers: according to the "cultural capital" we possess, according to the education we have received, and so on, music—especially what we Westerners call *great music*—is more or less accessible, or is strange, or incomprehensible . . . These sociological viewpoints are always necessary. But they answer only a *small part* of the questions posed above; they do not address the way that, implicitly or explicitly, *works configure in themselves their reception, their possible appropriation, even their listening.*

So it seems necessary to let the question of the *right to music* resound according to a somewhat different formulation: What place does a musical work assign to its listener? How does it require us to listen it? What means does it put *into play* to *compose a listening?* But also: What scope, what space for *play* does a work reserve, in itself, for those who play it or hear it, for those who *interpret it,* with or without instruments? How, through its own construction or architecture, does a musical work keep possibilities of active appropriation in its heart? Possibilities for adaptations or arrangements?

Who has a right to music? This question could be rephrased this way: What is, as it is outlined and destined in the works, the *subject* whom music addresses, or rather the one it *constructs*? And what falls to this subject as something *still to be done?* In other words: What must this listener-subject, subjected to music, do in order to *have a right* to it?

I will try to give a historical perspective to these questions, by retracing the joint and interdependent genesis of a certain *idea of work* and a certain *regime of listening* that responds to it. For that is the final horizon of this book: Where does the modern listener and his activity of listening come from? According to what necessities is this activity essentially determined in a figure of subjection to the work? And what reserves of other possible attitudes toward listening do these historical necessities harbor? Which is a way of saying that I will basically attempt a *critical history of listening.*

Who has a right to music? This question can also be reformulated thus: What can I make of music? What can I do *with* it? But also: What can I do *to it*, what can I do *to* music? What do I have the right to make *of*, do *with* or *to* music?

There is a field here that musicology has only very rarely taken seriously: I can *copy* (plagiarize, steal, divert) music; I can *rewrite* (adapt, arrange, transcribe) it; I can, finally and especially, *listen to it*. Schematically, I'll take the risk of regrouping these three possibilities under the generic term of *appropriation.*

(Interpretation, you will rightly point out, is also a form of appropriation of music. It is even, perhaps, the most important and most active form of this appropriation. But it seems to me that it is rarely interpretation *as such* that poses the question of the work *as such.* An interpretation that questions the very notion of a work would soon be qualified as adaptation or arrangement, a redirecting in the sense of a *rewriting.* But here it is a question—as I have said—of *questioning the very notion of a work*, and making this questioning the connecting thread leading to a critical history of listening.)

Who has a right to music? This question will be approached in three ways, in three historical and critical perspectives about the possible appropriation of music: (1) an archeology of politics and ideologies that imprint their mark on the apparatus of *copyright* and the *droit d'auteur*; (2) a reflection on the transformations in the practice of transcription or adaptation, in short, on the *place of arrangement* in musical life, mainly since Romanticism; (3) the sketching out of a *history of listening*, its organs and instruments.

If one had to gather together, condense these three approaches into a kind of allegory, the famous story told by Leopold Mozart could stand in this place: the allegory of Wolfgang, copying from memory Allegri's *Miserere*, for which performance and distribution rights were strictly reserved for the Sistine Chapel (as the performance rights of *Parsifal* would later be reserved for Bayreuth).[2] Mozart the father wrote to his wife:

> You may have heard talk of the famous *Miserere* of Rome, so esteemed that the musicians of the Chapel are forbidden, under penalty of excommunication, to let the smallest part of this piece go, to copy it or communicate it to anyone? Well, *we already have it* [emphasis in original]. Wolfgang wrote it down from memory, and we would have sent it to Salzburg with this letter if we didn't have to be present for its performance; but the way they perform it is more important than the composition itself, and so we will bring it home ourselves. Since it's one of the secrets of Rome, we don't want to confide it to strange hands *ut non incurremus mediate vel immediate in Censuram Ecclesiae* [so as not to run the risk, directly or indirectly, of censure from the Church]. (Letter dated April 14, 1770)

In other words, Mozart the son, whose incredible *auditory* capacities the father boasts of, could note down, that is, *copy* by listening to it, the "secret of Rome": not just the work itself but its *performance*, which thus became *transportable home*, torn from their reserved and guarded place. We can hear in these lines both the violence of a *right of listening* regulated by relationships of power, and the *phonographic* power of active, expert hearing (Wolfgang does a kind of "sampling" before the technology exists), its subversive force unleashed as soon as it is linked with a *technique* of inscription (pending that propagation that recording technology would bring).

Every right to listening both opens up and closes, that is to say *regulates* possibilities of *transfer* (as we say in the vocabulary of modern recording). But phonographic recording confers on these possibilities an unprecedented power, which *in law*, precisely, reverses the established judicial hierarchies.

With what could be called the *phonogrammatization* of music in general, listening has in effect experienced an unprecedented transformation, which its technical equipment provokes and reveals. We have to face facts: there has been rupture, alteration, in what we might call the *responsibility of listening*. It is no longer borne mainly by the musical *work*, by its *internal* categories (melodic or rhythmic patterns, prominent timbres or harmonic events, "signals" in all genres carefully arranged throughout its formal "envelope" in order to inscribe auditory "landmarks" there);[3] it has acquired a certain *autonomy*—it now has *instruments* (the disk, the sampler, the digital indexing of sound in general) to *act* on music. It no longer stems from a simple *reception* (or its semianagram: *perception*). Listening is *configuring* on its own, without being mainly subjected to a rhetorically articulated flux that orders it and structures it from the "interior" of the musical work.

From then on, we must look with a new light at this unusual responsibility of autonomous listening; we must think of the conditions and limits of the *right of the listener*.

If a certain regime of listening is perhaps in the process of coming to an end (and it is in fact to this ending that I would like to contribute), it remains for us to think about what listening means. I will argue at least that listening, insofar as it has a history, insofar as it is reflected and addressed, has always been *plastic*. Perhaps it is more so now than ever before.

CHAPTER 1

Author's Rights, Listener's Rights
(Journal of Our Ancestors)

I dream.

What if the listener I am were none other but the reincarnation of a distant predecessor?

What if the ears I have and carry everywhere with me were older than I am?

What if my two ears, which I sometimes outfit in headsets and other prostheses, had been prefabricated, at least in part, a long, long time ago?

To lend an ear, as they say, is of course to stretch it [*tendre l'oreille*, to listen, means literally "to stretch the ear"]; it is in a way to mimic internally the outer mobility of this organ among certain animal species. It is, even if all the while remaining motionless, to turn our attention toward what summons our listening.

But to lend an ear is also a matter of a *loan*. Or even a graft. I sense that these pinnae that I turn and turn back in me like antennae are to a large extent determined, in their internal movements, by a whole body of laws, by a *corpus* of which I am neither the master, nor the proprietor, nor the inventor: rather I inherit them, I receive them, I borrow them without even having chosen them. This ear that I lend is certainly above all lent to me.

By whom?

Answering that question would come down to investigating our distant predecessors, the innumerable listeners who preceded us who listen today. About our ancestors, about the movement of their pinnae, about their postures, I want to know everything. And for a long time I have accumulated for us their portraits and photographs (from medieval illuminations down to images from the cinema), where you can see them now absorbed or meditative, now suffering or seemingly transported. You are as familiar as I am with this family album, where we can see them arranging their bodies in order to listen. And letting themselves be arranged by it. One of our favorite scenes is the "cure by music," in which the sick man (a melancholic) receives sweet melodies through one ear as if the better to appease or chase away the ringing he seems to be suffering from in the other, which he supports with his open palm.[1]

As fascinating and engaging as this *(oto-)iconography* is, it tells me nothing, however, or very little, about what regulates musical listening *as such*. Of course it does allow me to see contexts, attitudes, positions of listening. But it necessarily remains silent about what directs these listenings, what prescribes them: it allows me to hear neither *what* those listeners heard, nor, more importantly, what they thought they *should be listening to*.

Should we turn to texts, to written testimonies? If so, which ones?

There are indeed, here and there, some collections that resemble precepts for listening. Like the wonderful *How to Listen* by Plutarch.[2] But generally they deal only with listening to a *discourse* (to a scholarly lecture, for instance); they do not concern *musical* listening. At least, to my knowledge, not before the twentieth century (and we will have to wonder why a "treatise" like "Instructions for Hearing New Music," by Adorno, could not see the light of day before a certain modernity . . .).[3]

There is also, of course, what we call music criticism, which, at least since Schumann or Berlioz, has oscillated between "objective" description of works and "subjective" description of the impressions they arouse. But whatever its interest and its sometimes virtuoso writing may be, this kind of criticism rarely makes its criteria explicit; above all, with a few exceptions, it does not question the notion of *the work*, which constitutes rather the presupposition or unspoken thought according to which it orients itself: the work is a whole, a given to which listening adapts itself. In fact, one could probably demonstrate that music criticism is born only at the moment when the notion of the musical work is stabilized: starting from the moment, then, when a certain change in the *regime of listening* (which I will try to define) has already occurred.

In order to investigate our duties as listeners, in order to question this *you must* that accompanies us, we will have to go back to the time before this transformation that turns musical listening into *listening-to-a-work*. For, along with the notion of the work, already a whole mass of criteria have infiltrated our ears, to be erased there as if they went without saying: listening to a work, that is to say also to its composer, my ear is already, more or less, regulated by an idea of "structure," it tries to grasp a whole that is articulated in parts . . . From then on, in order to circumscribe this modern regime of listening that Adorno could describe as "structural" (I will return to this), in order to convey the construction of values from which it rises, we have to let our ancestors speak from other places of discourse than those of criticism. We have to question them exactly where, for them, the work remains a *problem*, a subject for debate, even conflict.

That is why I invite you to follow me first into an investigation that will sometimes have the look of a *criminology* of listening.

Come, we're entering the courtroom.

Plagiarism and the Obligation of Truth

Now we are in the *hearing* rooms.

There are voices. Countless voices, each with its own complaint.

Choirs of voices that rise up from the transcripts of so many trials and debates that have been archived in the history of law.

What is their complaint?

This one, an ancient one, already speaks of plagiarism. Here we are hearing a certain Diagoras, philosopher and "composer," complaining of having been stripped of his inventions.[4] Here we hear Martial comparing his verses to his children and defining *plagiarius* (literally, "stealer of children") as someone who appropriates his writings:[5] a metaphor that has now vanished, since it has become so commonly used.

Closer to us, we can hear, in the midst of a choir of the faithful, the voice of Luther reading in archaic German the preface to his book of spiritual songs (*Geystliche Lieder*) of 1545:

I should . . . point out that the lied sung at funerals, "Nu last uns den leib begraben," bears my name, but is not by me; and my name should be removed from it [*und soll mein nam hinfurt davon gethan sein*]. Not because I reject it, for I like it very much, and it was a good poet who wrote it, named Johannes Weis . . . ; but I do not want to appropriate anyone else's work as my own [*sonder ich will niemand sein arbeit mir zu eigen*].[6]

Even before the first positive laws on copyright or the right of the author (the Statute of Queen Anne in 1710 in England and the decrees of 1791 and 1793 in France), some historians identify in all these voices the growing affirmation of an "obligation of truth" or a "right of name" that, after being applied to literature, slowly enters music. Even in the realm of church songs, which one might have thought was more inclined to communal anonymity.

A *duty of truth* . . . Ever since I read this expression by Hans-jörg Pohlmann, the great archaeologist of the "prehistory" of musical law,[7] it has not left me. Was that it, then, the *you must* that accompanies my listenings? Even when I make myself a little of the forger or plagiarist, even when I play you a record so you can hear *my* hearing, the idea of this obligation to truth does not let me go. It haunts me.

And I question myself. *To whom*, precisely, do I owe truth? To you, to the work, to the author? And the truth *of what*? Of the work, of my listening? On that subject our voices seem silent: they say nothing about us, about our ears.

Some people, like Johannes Mattheson, seem indeed to call upon us as witnesses. Or rather, this composer and theoreti-cian—whose works mark and record, at the beginning of the eighteenth century, a genuine turning point in the notion of originality in music—seems sometimes to be speaking *for us*, in our name. Especially when, in his *Kern melodischer Wissenschaft*, published in Hamburg in 1737, he forcefully asserts the value of *melody* alone: "The ear," he writes, "has more pleasure with a single, well-modulated voice than with twenty-four, in which the melody is so torn apart that we no longer know what it is trying to say."

It is indeed about my pleasure, about my ear, that Mattheson speaks when he supports his condemnation of counterpoint, when he emphasizes the value of well-formed melody over po-lyphony. And so it is by pointing me out as witness that he sets out his plea for originality (*inventio*, which for him is essentially melodic) in opposition to the work of contrapuntal *elaboration*: "Every good composer must be an original," he writes in his *Critica Musica* in 1722, before adding that "every *elaboratio*, beautiful as it may be, can be likened merely to interest, whereas *inventio* is like capital."

We are indeed the heirs of this economic metaphor, so true is it for us, even today, that the very notion of musical invention tends largely to be confused with that of a "good melody." Thus Mattheson contributes powerfully to *constructing* our ears by providing words and images for an evolution that, after him, will make the melodic idea the only real *capital of originality* of a composer. (As Carl Dahlhaus wrote so well: "The language used to discuss music directly affects the music as it represents itself in the listener's consciousness.")[8]

Nonetheless, despite all that our listenings, generally without knowing it, borrow from these notions of capital forged in the course of the history of the law of musicians, none of the voices we have encountered until now truly speaks about us: about what we do and, especially, what we have *the right to do* as we listen.

But let us keep lending an ear, in this vast hearing room. In the midst of the loudest voices that forge and hammer out the laws or categories regulating musical life, some are more discreet: those of our predecessors, those of our ancestors, simple lovers of music.

Here are a few journal entries—incomplete, discontinuous—where I have recorded these rare listeners for you.

1757: Music and Notes (at the Foot of the Page)

In 1757, not long after the publication of Mattheson's works, a certain Friedrich Wilhelm Zacharias, better known as a journalist than as an (amateur) composer, sent one of his compositions to Friedrich Wilhelm Marpurg, theoretician of music and editor of a journal on music. The parcel was accompanied by a letter that Marpurg also published, and which aroused a great deal of interest:

> It is with the greatest possible satisfaction [wrote Zacharias] that I delighted my eyes and ears with the enclosed symphony [his own!]; but, as soon as I had taken the bold decision to send it to you, my bad conscience awoke to reproach me for having, in the opening measures, copied something from a symphony by Mr. Graun. I could not say that this discovery was very pleasant for me, although copying Mr. Graun is in itself, as far as I am concerned, a merit.[9]

Zacharias, amateur composer, is delighted—a little bit the way I am—with his modest inventions. And it is at the moment when they are about to become *public*—he is sending them to Marpurg for publication—that the conscience of a *you must*, so close to my own, assails him. Like me, when I get ready to unveil to you the treasures pillaged and accumulated in the course of my listening campaigns, Zacharias, as he sends his symphony, feels he is *accountable*. Indebted. And that is why, in his letter, he echoes the opinion of his time on the question of musical plagiarism.

This opinion, in the realm of music, seems to him much more permissive than in the field of scholarly literature: "To my great surprise," he writes, "I hear it said that copying, in music, is regarded as an infraction that is less serious than in the realm of erudition [*in der Gelehrsamkeit*]." But, instead of consoling himself with this, Zacharias goes further; music, he says in brief, must be constrained to the same *obligation to truth* as erudition:

> They told me, to console me, that stealing a few bars from someone is a minor thing. Real boldness would be stealing

entire arias, entire symphonies. . . . I am surprised by this, and I should tell you that, in the realm of erudition, neither poets nor critics have gone so far. Poets especially try to assert their integrity in that, for the passages they copy, they give the original beneath their own lines. After that, it is no longer called copying, but imitating; and, with such poetry, the poet can make a fine show of his ability to "pillage" in every language, to be just at home in Greece as he is in England. Since I may be the first poet who, having been unable to quench his thirst for writing with poetry alone, sought aid from music, I would at least like to make myself famous by an invention liable to hold my fellow citizens—those gentlemen who copy music—to integrity. . . . We want . . . to be honest: the passages we copy from each other, we want to represent them in little notes under our pieces, with at the bottom the name of the composer from whom they were stolen. . . . That is the only way, by being the first to indicate the musical theft, that we could disarm the indiscreet memory of learned critics.

Thus, for Zacharias, one has only to acquit oneself from the obligation to truth by the scholarly indication of sources in order to be authorized to pillage whatever one likes. But Zacharias goes even further:

As I have already announced, I will soon print such an erudite musical work; for I want . . . to get the reputation for having been the first person in Germany, perhaps even in the world, to give compositions an appearance of erudition and to return its respectability to musical highway robbery [*musikalische Rauberey*].

Zacharias could well be, as he claims, the inventor of the (musical) notes at the bottom of the page. And maybe it is with him that the gathering of selected passages—an activity in which I am so ready to engage for you—becomes literally a *borrowing*, that is, a *quotation*: for this (unlike allusion or evocation) implies *exact* identification of the origin and ownership of the passage in question.

When I came upon the Zacharias letter for the first time, I exclaimed, not without joy: here is my first, my very first predecessor! How I loved reading and rereading these lines! I didn't know a note of his symphony, or of his other *music-loving* works, that is to say the works of this amateur-collector *maniac of melodies*; but I could already imagine them, teeming with notes at the bottom of the page, an immense potpourri of his borrowings as a listener! They resembled the masterpiece I dream of, that suite articulating my best, favorite moments. And I could recognize myself in him, I who, almost always, note down somewhere the beautiful passages that I think I can borrow to send them to you in my name.

What a difference, I said to myself, between this listener's voice and that of a Mattheson who, barely excusing fortuitous reminiscences in others' works, strongly condemned deliberate, intentional borrowings: "It sometimes occurs by chance," he wrote in his *Volkommene Capellmeister* of 1739, "that one chances upon . . . ways that others have already traveled . . . without having chosen them expressly"; before adding that it isn't fitting to proceed thus "on purpose," or worse, "to put down in writing a catalogue of such scraps."

Now as you know, I have too many catalogues of scraps. In any case, you can at least testify better than anyone that my borrowings are *always* intentional; it is always on purpose that I draw from passages in my musical library that I have spotted in advance, for you. Evidently Mattheson, like so many others, would not like the minute, sometimes obsessive listener that I am. Listening, I take notes, I scribble down words, timing, track or measure numbers, logograms: I keep noting my reference marks, cataloguing, indexing my listener's borrowings.

In short, if the criterion of intention or premeditation of the borrowing unquestionably makes Mattheson a precursor of the modern *author's* rights, it seems to me, on the other hand, that the music-loving joy of the *listener* Zacharias makes him truly an ancestor of the discophiles we are.

And yet, once my enthusiasm is over, I don't really find myself in him. It is not as a scholar that I like to send you my listenings. When Zacharias writes, "There will be, perhaps, people presumptuous enough to pass us off as minds of little invention or imagination, but no one could question our reputation for great culture," I can't really associate myself with that *us*. We, you and I, are not there. For we don't really have much to do with erudition. What we want, simply, is for others to recognize a status in our listenings, even the most naïve ones, even the least "scholarly" ones. That people recognize them as inventions, not *of* the work, but *in* the work. Which, at bottom, may have nothing to do with collages or potpourris, with the streams of quotations of that strange listener-composer-amateur . . .

1835: A Great Change in Our Customs

If the chronology of my journal is more than fragmentary, if its geography is fickle, leaping from country to country, it is because, as I have said, the listener's voices that manage to make themselves heard in our hearing room are exceptional. But every time they are fascinating, if one manages to capture them.

Here is the voice of a lawyer, a certain Antoine Lefebvre. He pleads in the first person plural, he says "we," he associates *us* implicitly in his diagnosis:

> A great change has occurred in our customs. . . . We no longer go to the theater, as before, to hear the poem, to identify with the more or less moving incidents of the plot; it is only for the music, and even only for a few outstanding pieces, that we go to lyric spectacles. We are inclining to the customs of Italy, where the spectator has card parties in his box with his friends

while he waits for the currently fashionable aria, without both-ering in the least about the subject of the libretto.[10]

What is he talking about?

He is pleading for his clients, directors of the Opéra and the Opéra-Comique. They have filed a complaint against a concert organizer, a man named Masson de Puitneuf, who in 1833 had formed an orchestra that gave evening concerts outside on the Champs-Élysées; his repertory included, along with contradances and variations, arias taken from the most popular operas being performed in Parisian theaters. Public success was considerable. Thus the directors of the great lyric stages tried to oppose this undertaking, which they saw as dangerous competition. The law-yer continues:

> If the organizers of public concerts are allowed to unveil still-recent musical novelties, and can thus satisfy the dominant taste of the day at low cost, it is obvious that these merchants will unfailingly ruin the great lyric theaters. The court should not have any illusions about the importance of the decision it is summoned to hand down: the fate of music in France is in the balance.

The stakes, beyond even the dramatic rhetoric of a lawyer's pleading, are in fact high. For, through *our* right as listeners, because of the licit or illicit nature of *our* attitudes of listening, it was a question, neither more nor less, of protecting the *integrity* of the works performed on stage; that is to say, not letting them disintegrate into selected extracts according to the caprices of taste.

Masson's lawyer retorted in vain that his client was offering only simple "public readings" rather than actual *representations* of the operas in question; the court ruled in favor of the theater directors, judging that "the composer, who sells a printed score, gives and intends to give an enjoyment that is exclusive to the buyer alone"; that is to say that the buyer is not authorized "to exploit the music sold." This decision, which was made in 1835, is of the highest importance for the future of musical life. And it is not insignificant that it was made in our name; or rather, with the declared objective of also legislating our habits as listeners.

In fact, with this verdict, part of a movement that began with the revolutionary laws of 1791 and 1793, there is a *shift of music toward the paradigm of theater*. While, during the time of Mattheson and Zacharias, musical law was essentially conceived according to the model of literature, the French Revolution made it swing over to the side of the theater. A major event, it can be read explicitly in the title of the famous decree of January 13–19, 1791, relative "to theaters and to the right of representation and performance of *dramatic and musical* works" (emphasis mine). This decree, which still forms the cornerstone of our judicial apparatus, stipulates in its third article: "Works by living authors cannot be represented in any public theater, throughout all of France, without the formal written consent of the authors."

Still, until our 1835 trial, an uncertainty persisted concerning works given without *staging*. Once this uncertainty was removed by the 1835 decision, which created a legal precedent, one could regard *every musical interpretation* as a *representation*, subject as such to the authorization of the author. This opened the way, after that—and this is what makes it important for us—to the infiltration, in the musical field, of a tradition that had long been confined to the theater: *authorial interpretation*, that is, authorized (supervised) by the author.[11]

So long as our ear was implicitly regulated according to a judicial concept of music modeled on literature, interpretation as such did not constitute a problem *of law*. The best testimony of this is that of an English judgment of 1777, involving Johann Christian Bach. He had filed a complaint against the publishers James Longman and Charles Lukey, whom he accused of having printed and sold copies of his works without his authorization.[12] The judge, Lord Mansfield, ruled in his favor in these terms: "An individual can use a copy by playing it; but he has no right to strip the author of his profit, by multiplying the copies and using them for his own purposes."

This decision is indeed important from the point of view of the history of law: after the very first law on copyright—the Statute of Queen Anne in 1710, which attributed the ownership of copies of "books and other writings" to their authors for a limited period[13]—it is the verdict in favor of Bach that allows the clarification that music was indeed included in "other writings" ("music . . . can be written down and ideas are conveyed in it by means of signs and marks," declared Mansfield). But the fact remains that interpretation was purely and simply distanced from the field of law ("an individual can use a copy by playing it"); that is to say, it was withdrawn from all *right of inspection* by the composer.

Thus it is only after the French precedent of 1835 that the *interpretation* of music (of *all* music, whether or not it is staged) could little by little be integrated into the judicial sphere of the *authority of the author.*

This change *in law*—that our ears will end up noting—signified that the author henceforth had the judicial means to supervise the conformity of the interpretations of his works. That was the case for a long time in the field of theater,[14] and it is thanks to the revolutionary decree of 1791, then to its explicit expansion in 1835, that the notion of authorial interpretation could truly *take shape* [prendre corps] in music.

1853: A Listener in Court

There is at least one unusual listener who, about twenty years later, came forward to testify that our ears have *incorporated* this notion.

The listener in question, a certain Count Thadée Tyszkiewicz,[15] did not hesitate to take to court, *in the name of the author,* those who infringed on the new rule of respect for works (in this case,

Weber's *Freischütz*). He instituted, in the most serious way possible, a "suit for damages" against the Imperial Academy of Music, that is, the Opéra.

I know almost nothing about this strange count (except that he was a critic for the *Leipziger musikalische Zeitung*); but I read his complaint, published by the *Gazette des tribunaux* on December 8, 1853, with an astonishment mingled with *recognition*:

> Having arrived in Paris last Thursday, I leaped for joy when I saw posted an announcement for a performance of the *Frey-schutz* [*sic*] at the Imperial Academy of Music. . . . One of the first to enter the hall, I went over in my head all the perform-ances of this opera I have attended, savoring even the imper-fections I had had to suffer through, in the conviction that what I was about to hear would amply recompense me. . . . The feelings I had while I entered the hall were succeeded first of all by a kind of stupor. I thought I was under the sway of a bad dream, the butt of a practical joke. . . . I had just heard a vocal and instrumental mess unprecedented in the musical an-nals of the countries I had till now traveled through. . . . Until then at least Weber's score had been played in its entirety. The curtain rose for the third time. Instead of the third act, they gave scraps of the third act, scraps sewn together without the slightest concern for stage design, without the least musical feeling, a ridiculous potpourri. Agathe's prayer was cut; the hermit's song, Ottokar's song, Max's narration—so heart-breaking, so real—as well as the chorus, "Always was he a villain!"—all cut, all! My indignation was at its height. I won-dered where the conductor had gone to discover the unspeak-able feeling an artist must have to set his hand to carrying out such a sacrilege! I wondered where M. Roqueplan [Nestor Roqueplan, director of the Opéra], a dealer in stage produc-tions, had gone to look for the right to falsify his merchandise publicly, to weigh it on crooked scales, to insult me, the audience! . . . .

. . . P.S.: I have brought a suit for damages against the Imperial Academy of Music. The thousand voices of the press will make the facts to be revealed by the investigation resound throughout the entire world.

The long complaint of this surprising listener was in fact widely disseminated in the French and foreign press. Although he was represented by a lawyer named Lachaud, famous for his art of "sentimental pleading," our count had few chances to win his suit. Henry Celliez, lawyer for the Opéra, demanded 3,000 francs in damages from the impudent listener who had tarnished the reputation of the company. After that, before the Civil Court of the Seine, in December 1853, Maître Lachaud pleaded in these terms:

Our situation, then, is as sad as possible; not only has my client had his ears injured, but he will pay for having dared to complain. . . . Looking at it this way, M. Roqueplan will become a millionaire.

This affair is unique in the history of law: a listener complains of the harm done to his organs by a performance that is disrespectful of the author and the work. Previously, in fact, the cuts and falsifications that so offended our count were given value and attributed to the skill of the *arranger*, central figure of musical life.

Thus, in 1824, François Henri Joseph Blaze (called Castil-Blaze) had arranged the "same" *Freischütz* as *Robin des bois* [*Robin Hood*], transposing the action to England and inserting into the score extracts from another opera by Weber, *Euryanthe* (which he himself had reorchestrated, having at his disposal only a version for piano . . .). The first *Robin des bois* was a fiasco; but one week later, Castil-Blaze presented a *new version*, which had considerable success and popularized the music of Weber, giving rise to new arrangements for piano with titles like *Le Franc chasseur* [*The Free Hunter*], *La Fiancée du chasseur* or *Le Chasseur noir* . . . For this reversal in the public fortune of the work, Castil-Blaze had a ready-made explanation: its first version, too close to Weber's original, wasn't well enough adapted to the taste of the French public!

The fact remains that, when Weber stayed in Paris in 1826, he could hear that a shortened version of the hunters' chorus was sung even in the churches, with an adapted text: *Chrétien diligent / Devance l'aurore* . . . Weber complained in vain about the treatment inflicted on his work—"Ah! Monsieur," he wrote in an open letter to Castil-Blaze reprinted in several newspapers at the time, "what will become of all that is sacred to us . . . ?"—but the legislation of the 1820s and the absence of international agreements on copyright made his protests useless. Above all, it seems that the ears of the public ("us") still had nothing to do with the *authorial* values that would be imposed later on.

In the 1840s, attitudes about the same work had changed considerably. When they decided to stage another production of *Freischütz* at the Opéra in 1841, the director, Léon Pillet, turned to Berlioz; not to "adjust" a work to the demands of French taste (although he could not say no to the addition of a ballet), but rather to get around the impossibility of representing on this stage works that included spoken dialogue. A passage from Berlioz's *Memoirs* speaks better than any commentary on the restriction involved in the adaptability of a work:

I had just returned from [a] long peregrination in Germany, when M. Pillet, the Director of the Opéra, formed the plan of getting up the *Freischütz* for the stage. . . . The spoken text had to be put into recitative. M. Pillet offered me this task.

"I do not think," I answered, "that the recitatives you wish for ought to be added to the *Freischütz* at all. However, since it can only be performed at the Opéra on that condition, and as you would probably, if I declined the task, give it to someone less familiar with Weber than myself, and certainly less devoted to the glorification of his masterpiece, I accept your offer on one condition: the work shall be played exactly as it is, without any alteration either in the book or the music."

"That is my intention," replied M. Pillet. "Do you think me capable of renewing the scandal of *Robin des Bois*?"

"Very well; in that case I shall set to work."[16]

We can see a change from the *castilblazades* (as they were then called) of the 1820s: in the statements attributed to the director of the Opéra, they had become a "scandal"; and Berlioz's activity as arranger is minimized, erased, for the sake of the "masterpiece" it must serve. It is even in order to *avoid something worse* that Berlioz accepts the task offered him: he arranges the work only in order to limit the space of arrangement, to prevent as much as possible attacks on the original, which he calls *derangements*: "The feeling which had urged me to insist on the preservation of Weber's work in its integrity, a feeling which many would call fetishism, removed all pretext for the manipulations, derangements, suppressions, and corrections, which otherwise would have been eagerly made" (345).

Berlioz, however, himself acknowledged that rigidity in dealing with the work has its disadvantages too: "But one serious drawback was a necessary result of my obstinacy: the spoken dialogue, when set *entirely* to music, seemed too long, notwithstanding all my precautions to render it as concise as possible" (345; emphasis mine [translation slightly altered]). Berlioz's position, then, is still unstable. Even if we should count him among the most ardent defenders of respect for the work (as testified by other passages from his *Memoirs*, which we will read later on), his discourse is below the level of Wagner's, for example. An article published in the *Revue et gazette musicale* in May 1841, just before the premiere of the *Freischütz* arranged by Berlioz, foretold its failure: Weber's opera was a "complete whole" and the insertion of the recitatives could only harm it, asserted the article's author, who was none other than Wagner himself.

Wagner's predictions turned out to be correct, but probably for reasons entirely other than his own. After twelve performances, the work was withdrawn from public performance. To recoup the production expenses, it served in the ensuing years as a "curtain raiser" for ballets, shortened and cut so that it could better fulfill this new function . . .

If arrangement, in Berlioz, becomes a last resort (to which one must, if I dare say it, adapt), it is because it is henceforth *weighed* against the original. Unlike an older concept, which had not yet made adaptation a competition that threatened the work on its own terrain,[17] we see in Berlioz the beginnings of a turning toward a concept we can describe as *substitutive*: starting from the moment when the arrangement is understood as being able, if necessary, *to replace* the original, its space of lawfulness shrinks like Balzac's magic donkey skin; it becomes precisely a *counterfeit*. If we see this new concept emerging, especially in Berlioz, it is still a matter of a more general phenomenon, whose consequences we will soon discover.

The fact remains that, to listen to our count, in 1853, the *Freischütz*, to be able to be heard *legitimately*, had to remain intact, as it was. To his ears, the music began to lose something of the elasticity, of the *plasticity*, that it had had before, letting the modern ideal of the *work* emerge.

The final decision of the court in the Tyszkiewicz affair was not a decision: the case was dismissed and the plaintiff made to bear the expenses. That is why we can say that this trial, like so many others, is notable more from the publicity it was given than from its legal outcome. Which does not mean—far from it—that it did not have any consequences: Weber's opera would be withdrawn from the repertoire of the Opéra for more than twenty years, until 1876. That is the most visible, if I dare say it, result of this affair, which was both exceptional and exemplary in so many respects.

But, for us, this listener's complaint had lasting and profound effects (although hard to measure): by giving voice, *our* voice, to the ideals of respect for the work and authorial interpretation, it contributed—one piece of evidence among so many others in a vast historical trial underway—to making us, from one point of view, *critical* listeners.

1841: Our Portrait in a Cartoon

From another point of view, however, the increasing restriction of music's adaptability—its rigidification into *oeuvres*, if you like—goes along with, and gives rise to, a concomitant reduction of its *critical space*.

That is what this image I have pasted into our journal shows. You will recognize a caricature of us in the process of listening to a "Grrrreat performance of the Grrrreat Stabat Mater" (by Rossini); we are provided with scrolls that give us thoughts and the following words: "Aren't you dancing the Stabat Mater, then?" "Is that a Stabat? My, how it dances"; "I can't wait for the end . . . it's carrying me away."

What are they making us say, and why?

To understand how our private thoughts as listeners are dependent on a *polemology* of listening, we must briefly restore the context of this image.[18]

In the 1830s, Rossini, ill, hardly ever left his villa in Bologna. One of the rare trips he took led him in 1831 to Madrid, where he was the guest of Don Manuel Fernandez Varela, a high Spanish dignitary and a fervent admirer of Rossini's music. In this man's home, Rossini wrote a draft of his *Stabat Mater*; but he soon cut short his visit, promising to send the work to Varela once it was finished. During a trip to Paris the following year, he wrote six movements of the twelve he had planned. A friend of Rossini's, the composer Giovanni Tadolini, completed the work and sent it to Varela with a dedication. Varela thanked

Rossini with a gift of great value, and had the *Stabat Mater* performed in Madrid in 1833.

When Varela died in 1841, the Parisian publisher Aulagnier acquired the manuscript at an auction. He prepared to publish it, but Troupenas, the publisher of Rossini's works in France,[19] having heard a rumor of this plan, did everything he could to prevent its execution. He had Rossini sign a contract by which the composer yielded him exclusive rights to publish the six original movements of *Stabat Mater*, and certified that he had never yielded the rights to anyone before. Rossini then undertook to finish the six allographic movements himself. Aulagnier, however, let it be known that he considered the dedication to Varela, as well as the gift Varela had given to Rossini in exchange, as a veritable contract of sale; and he threatened to present the *Stabat Mater* at a "monster-concert," in case the right to publish it was refused him.

The affair ended up in several jurisdictions, until a verdict passed by the Civil Court of the Seine in January 1842 explicitly rejected the interpretation of the dedication as a proper form of sale. After that, Aulagnier, who had been associated with the publisher Schlesinger, resorted to questionable methods to discredit the work that had slipped through his hands and tried to prove that there was nothing truly "sacred" in its style (that it was scarcely different from the operas and other "secular" works by the same author).

The methods and objectives of Aulagnier and Schlesinger are indefensible. They had the melodies of the *Stabat Mater* arranged into waltzes and other contradances, while at the same time inserting notices in the *Revue et gazette musicale* such as "Very graceful dances, waltzes, gallops, on themes of Rossini's Stabat Mater are now in vogue here" (April 24, 1842), and "They have just published quadrilles in London based on the tunes from this work. Without a doubt, Rossini wrote the 'Stabat Mater' to please those who organize balls and public entertainments" (December 4, 1842).

What interests me, beyond the initial paltry motivations of Aulagnier and Schlesginer, is that the arrangements they gave rise to were for many people part of what is still today one of the most serious *critical* questions for the musicology of Rossini: to find out if the work is truly "sacred" in its style, and to what extent it differed from "lighter" works made for the stage.[20]

Here is the title page of one of these arrangements, published by Aulagnier, where Rossini's name is conspicuous by its absence: "Anecdotal, enigmatic, allegorical, funny, comic, *critical* [emphasis mine], caustic, epigrammatic, satiric, historical, and veridical quadrille on motifs of orphan excerpts from the Stabat Mater dedicated to Fernandez Varela." It is on the lithography decorating this page that we can read the scrolls that make us instruments of a polemics that is revolting in many respects. But, if we disregard the motivations in this struggle, we can begin to realize that *a form of polemology always haunts our listenings.* That they are used here to serve such a cause is no accident, nor is it a stroke of ill luck. And if we are more readily tempted to take the side of someone like Tyszkiewicz, we should not forget that his pleading for the *work* is also a taking by violence—only he is lending his ears to another camp in the battle.

The difference between the opposing forces is not so much, as we are tempted to think, that one is right or law-abiding (the work and the author), and the other dishonest. It is rather that, on Tyszkiewicz's side, the polemical nature of listening is forgotten, erased when faced with the allegedly self-evident values of authenticity and authorship. But this erasure of the polemology that always paralyzes our organs is part of a complex tendency by which the critical force of listening, like that of arrangement, is restrained and denied.

CHAPTER 2 *Writing Our Listenings: Arrangement, Translation, Criticism*

—ARRANGEMENT. Transformation of a text to make possible its performance for another category of instruments than those for which it had been written. . . . Our era is fertile in sacrileges committed for the radio, the cinema, and the ballet (cf. Chopin's "Tristesse"). Here again, a stricter vocabulary should be used: the erudite high style of what Bach wrote should be called *arrangement,* while *adaptation* (since this word has a more common flavor than the other) should be used for the misappropriation of property practiced by so many philistines.

Encyclopédie de la musique (Paris: Fasquelle, 1958)

I love them more than all the others, the arrangers. The ones who sign their names *inside* the work, and don't hesitate to set their name down next to the author's. Bluntly adding their surname by means of a *hyphen*: Beethoven-Liszt (for a piano version of the nine symphonies), Bach-Webern (for an orchestration of the *ricercar* in the *Musical Offering*), Brahms-Schoenberg, Schubert-Berio, who else—in short, a whole mass of double-barrel signatures.

Now, it seems to me that what arrangers are signing is above all a listening. *Their* hearing of a work. They may even be the only listeners in the history of music to *write down* their listenings, rather than *describe* them (as critics do). And that is why I love them, I who so love to listen to someone listening. I love hearing them hear.

One of my most fascinating listening experiences is listening to an orchestration or transcription of a work that I think I know well. Bach's Toccata and Fugue in D minor, for instance. To say that I know it is an understatement. I could, like many others, whistle or sing pages and pages of it. And yet what a surprise, the day I listened to it in Stokowski's orchestration! You can say what you like about it: that it is kitsch, that it turns Bach's organ into music for costume dramas . . . Perhaps. But what fascinates me is the unique experience of listening to such an arrangement: my ear is continually pricked up, torn between the actual orchestra and the imaginary organ that keeps superimposing itself like the shadow of a memory. I hear, inseparably, *both* the organ screened by the orchestra *and* the orchestra screened by a phantom organ. That, I think, is the strength of every arrangement: *we are hearing double.* In this oscillating, divided listening, in this listening that lets itself be hollowed out by the endlessly traversed gap between the original version and its deformation in the mirror of the orchestra, what I hear in some way is that the originality of the original receives its own place from its being put to the test of *plasticity.*

For what happens to it, what happens to Bach in the hands of Stokowski, is truly a *plastic* experience. The notes that had been destined for the organ are here stretched or compressed, they are endowed with a new *weight:* the orchestra draws them toward registers where they are *counterbalanced,* where they gain more heaviness or lightness: they become weightier by passing through the grainy filter of the basses, they are diffracted in the subtle blending of flutes and harps . . . In short, I am experiencing the test of elasticity, of the *plasticity* of a Toccata that I thought I knew. Not only am I continuously listening to Bach from the auditory perspective that Stokowski gives me of it (in the distance from which he lets me desire the original), but also, conversely, I cannot hear Stokowski without being struck by Bach's organ that pulls me by the ear. There is, if not a reciprocity (for the relationship is not symmetrical), at least a fascinating form of oscillation.

In comparison to what I so like in him when he arranges and deforms, however, Stokowski's spoken discourse is disappointing. Let us listen to him, interviewed in 1962, explain the motivations of his orchestration:

> I had . . . the feeling that music lovers should hear this music. Of course, they sometimes hear it at church; but the thousands of people who go to symphony concerts should hear it too. So I orchestrated it, trying to give the same impression of music, to transmit the same message, the same inspiration, through the modern orchestra.[1]

It is strange that, in 1962, during the era of mass recording, Stokowski can declare that, in order to spread Bach's organ work, we have to pass it through a transcription *for orchestra*. Strange, too, for our ears paralyzed by authenticity, that he can think he has transmitted, with such a swollen orchestration, the "same impression" as the original. One is reminded more of Hollywood, or of Disney (in fact, it is this orchestration that Stokowski directed for the soundtrack of the famous *Fantasia*).[2] In any case, no one today would go so far as to argue that it is the "same message," the "same inspiration" as in Bach.

Whatever the case, Stokowski the arranger hides behind respect. He crosses out his own signature by erasing himself, pretending that he is only rendering a service. In this, he joins the chorus of all those who, in arrangement, see above all a *function* in the service of the original, which he is often summoned temporarily to *replace*.

Such a concept goes along with and justifies what we will have to call the *decline of arrangement*, a practice that Berlioz already regarded as a sometimes inevitable last resort and that, after him, sound recording would make even more unjustifiable: why orchestrate the organ, why reduce the orchestra to the piano, when the phonograph is capable of transporting and spreading everywhere what is in effect the *original*?

Thus, according to the article on "arrangement" by Malcolm Boyd in the *New Grove Dictionary of Music and Musicians* (1980), the decline of arrangement is due especially to two so-called external factors: on one hand, copyright, which forbids the adaptation and arrangement of protected musical works without prior permission from the author; on the other hand, radio and the gramophone, which "have largely replaced the piano transcription as a disseminator of the chamber, orchestral and operatic repertory." I will not go back over the first of these "factors," the legal one, which I am surprised at being so quickly described as "external." As for the second one, it testifies to a concept of arrangement as a means of *transmission*, as a method of *communication* of the original, for which it is *substituted* from then on.

I will try to demonstrate to what extent such a (practical) concept of arrangement is the result of a *wrong* reading of its golden age, that is, the Romantic era. We will see on the contrary that, in Schumann or Liszt especially, *the original and the arrangement are complementary, contiguous in their incompleteness and their distance from the essence of the work.* And that this essence (the Idea, if you like), far from being given in advance, must remain always yet to come, at the (endless) end of the different adaptations. In other words: the essence of the work (in a certain sense: the original) is *at the* (endless) *end* rather than at the beginning. That also means that this essence or idea must, in order to remain yet to come, be able not to be assured, not to be proven; it must let itself be haunted by the threat of its disappearance. If there is a work (which must remain an hypothesis), it exists at the *risk* of arrangement.

It is from this Romantic moment that I will try to extract the *critical* (and not practical) necessity of arrangement. For although Romantic arrangement corresponds to a hyperbolic concept of the work, we must never lose sight of the fact that this is understood as an experience, or better: as a never completed *test*, always begun again. For the arrangers that Liszt and Schumann are, for these remarkable listeners who *sign and write down their listenings*, the Work is never already given: infinitely deferred, it oscillates between appropriation (translation) and disappropriation (criticism). That is why they have so much to tell us about the forces that are sleeping in our organs, covered over by the values of authenticity or respect. If we are to believe Liszt and Schumann, we might begin to envisage our listenings as *writing*, or even as *rewriting*.

Ever Since There Have Been Works . . .

Arrangement, then, will essentially be for us the paradigm of a critical, active relationship with *works*. Which, at least in music, *do not exist as such* before the eighteenth century.

True, the Latin word for work, *opus*, seems to embed this notion firmly in distant eras. But this word, before the meaning it ended up taking on in modern musical publishing ("Opus" number *X* of composer *Y*), did not signify simply or solely our "oeuvre." The Latin *opus* is both the work and its result. So it is indeed the work in the sense of the work of art, but it is also the activity (the work underway in the sense of *to be at work*) that leads to the work. In a passage in the *Musica* that the Kapellmeister Nikolaus Listenius published in 1549 in Nuremberg,[3] we find these two competing definitions: "practical music" [*praktike*], he writes, is expressed in an *opus* (in the sense of action, performance, work), although no *opus* (this time in the sense of work of art) remains after the performance; while "poetic music" [*poietike*], not content with practice [*exercitio*] alone, delivers after the work a "complete and finished" [*consummatum et effectum*] *opus*, that is, even after the death of the "maker" [*artifice mortuo*], a "perfect and absolute *opus*" [*opus perfectum et absolutum*]. Although this text (and especially this final expression) has often been interpreted as indicating the existence of a notion of a work independent of its performance and subsisting in itself, we must, however, wait until the end of the eighteenth century not only for this notion to be translated into musical life, but also for it to become little by little, over the course of the nineteenth century, a kind of *regulating idea*.[4] And the consolidation of the notion of musical work went through faster or slower sedimentation depending on the country and on musical genres.

If we are to believe the testimony of Charles Burney, an English musicographer who traveled to Germany and the Netherlands in 1772, musical performance in Berlin was subject to surveillance on the part of the King of Prussia that foreshadows Berlioz's attitude fifty years later:

> In the opera house, as in the field, his majesty is such a rigid disciplinarian, that . . . if any of his Italian troops dare to deviate from strict discipline, by adding, altering, or diminishing a single passage in the parts they have to perform, an order is sent, *de par le Roi*, for them to adhere strictly to the notes written by the composer, at their peril.[5]

Now, for the English observer that Burney is, this attitude is not in the least self-evident: "That is why," he writes, "music has not changed one iota in this country, since H.M. tolerates freedom in art no more than he does in matters of government." We can understand the surprise and reservations felt by Burney—who had traveled through France and Italy two years before—if we measure how long it was before this law of fidelity to the work was imposed elsewhere, even in other parts of Germany. It is this kind of *policing of performance* that Berlioz, in *The Art of Music and Other Essays*, demands for Paris, under the guise of a discussion of the exotic and romanticized "musical customs" of China:

> The Chinese lawmakers impose severe penalties, rightly, I think, not only on theater directors who stage K'ung Fu-tze's operas badly, but also on singers who give unworthy performances of excerpts at concerts. . . . If a singer is judged guilty of the offense of desecration I have just mentioned, she is given a first warning by having her left ear cut off. If she repeats the mistake, she loses her right ear as a second warning.[6]

Berlioz himself admits that "Chinese law" in this case "seems too severe," since "a perfect performance could hardly be expected from a singer who has no ears." But, beyond the slightly facile humor grafted onto bogus exoticism, we can hear in these lines to what point surveillance of musical performance is a matter *of ears*. And above all, we can deduce from this that such a "law," even in less drastic forms, did not exist in Paris or elsewhere. Berlioz's *Memoirs* abound in remarks on such-or-such Parisian flutist who, so that he "could be heard," transposed his part "to a higher octave, thus destroying the result the author had hoped for"; or else on the "first oboe" in the Dresden orchestra who, despite his "beautiful sound," was reproached for his "old style," that is to say, his "craze for doing *trills* and *mordents*," which "outraged" Berlioz as an author directing his work.[7]

Italian musical life seems to have been the most resistant to the modern ideal of the work. As Liszt writes, testifying to his experience of the Italian public in his *Lettres d'un bachelier ès musique*:

> We enjoy music and performance, the abstraction made from the poetic given: we never lose the singer into the character he represents: we always know perfectly that it is . . . Mr. Petrazzi and not Othello that we're dealing with. Thus the Italians find

it quite simple to applaud the actors after a thrust of the sword or during the most tragic scenes.[8]

In other words, the actor-singer does not so much *play* a role following the indications of the work; he *is* the character, especially since the role is thought up *in the first place for a certain actor.* That is why Gaetano Donizetti, in 1845, can write: "As for the subject [of an upcoming opera], I will do *Onore vince Amore.* Lablache [bass] *is* an old, respectable man of about sixty years. La Persiani [soprano] *is* a young woman under guardianship [etc.]."[9]

Even before the opera in question is written, it is already such or such a singer who *is* the character, instead of the role existing *absolutely*, as we would tend to think of it today, simply to be *played* as well as possible by the interpreter who embodies it. As soon as roles are thus destined for an actual singer before they even exist, as soon as they are indissolubly linked with interpreters (who are, moreover, by the same token, not yet simple *intermediaries*), we can see why every new performance of the opera, in another theater and with another company, is, if not a new creation, at least a labor of *adjustments* (aggiustamenti) sometimes leading to a considerable reorganization of the original material.[10]

The composer himself often entrusted these *aggiustamenti* to someone in whom he had confidence, a kind of *authorial proxy.* Thus a letter dated December 1843 bears witness to the way Donizetti felt he could entrust Mercadante with preparing a version of his opera *Caterina Cornaro* for Naples; he asks his on-site substitute purely and simply to appropriate the work: "Correct all the mistakes in my score, keep a watchful eye on my opera, do anything you deem useful with it—in the strongest sense of the word: add to the instrumentation, rewrite the instrumentation, lighten it, shorten, lengthen, transpose, in short: make it your own work."[11]

Such an *operative* practice (since we cannot speak of a "work" here in the sense we understand the word today) was upheld longer in Italian opera than in other fields of European musical life. With the consequence that Berlioz describes ironically in *The Art of Music and Other Essays*: "Common sense would say that . . . the singers are there for the operas; the fact is just the other way around—the operas are there for the singers. A score must continually be fitted, recast, patched up, lengthened, or shortened" (58).

The distance is great between such a practice and our modern concept of the score, for which Liszt still had to fight in 1835 when he called for the foundation of a kind of Museum of Musical Works. These words of Liszt's seem to say in advance what *our* vision, *today*, would be, about a "musical heritage":

> In the name of all musicians, in the name of art and social progress, we request . . . the foundation of a competition once every five years for religious, dramatic, and symphonic music. The best compositions in these three genres should be solemnly performed for a month at the Louvre, and then acquired and published at government expense. In other words—the foundation of a new MUSEUM.[12]

Respect for musical works, their preservation, their inclusion in a national heritage, subventions for the creation of musical works, competitions for composition: all these demands, whose novelty and pertinence in 1835 we can have some sense of, are now ours (even if they are periodically called into question). In fact, the eighth point that Liszt proposes describes very precisely the contemporary regime of our musical life:

> Eighthly, the publication at low cost of the most remarkable works of all ancient and modern composers, from the Renaissance of music to the present day . . . could have the title

MUSICAL PANTHEON. The biographies, essays, commentaries, and explanatory notes which should accompany it will make up a veritable ENCYCLOPEDIA of music.

Even if the notion of a musical work (the *opus perfectum* in the sense of Listenius) has existed for a long time, its *implementation*, or *mise en oeuvre*, if I may put it this way, was the result of a construction, of a *museum edification* that played out between 1770 (for Prussia) and 1850 (for Italy). We are its heirs, we who hear works today, who listen to "the" *Magnificat* by Bach, "the" *Don Giovanni* of Mozart (more or less well embodied on stage by one singer or another) . . .

So it is these works that direct, attract, or flesh out my desire for listening and my desire to make you hear them, that is to say to hear you hear. In a sense, there are nothing but works for us. Which are not necessarily written, notated, and signed by one single person (I listen to recordings, sounds, improvisations, sonorous pillagings . . .), but which are always works, to the precise extent that I want to *rehear* them and make you *re-listen* to them. Even (or especially) partially. My idea of a beautiful passage or a chosen excerpt can only be understood starting from the work itself.

When I get to speak to you again, soon, about arrangements as I dream of them for us, ever since the horizon opened by Liszt and Schumann, it will be in the sense of the arrangement of a *work*. But without enclosing them in a *functionalist* horizon.

Functions of Arrangement

We could attempt a systematic analysis of the various *functions* that arrangement is supposed to fulfill (I will do so only schematically, the better to forget them, in a way). Which would come down to sketching out a "systematics of deformation" of musical works, as Antoine Berman did for the translation of literary works.[13] (The recurrent analogy between arrangement and translation still awaits us: I will return to it, with Liszt.)

Beyond its social or public functions of *communication* and *diffusion* (the work for orchestra is supposed to circulate more easily in a piano reduction), we should analyze other functions of arrangement, such as those we might call *clarifying* and *corrective*.

The extreme example of clarification is that of the "setting words to the music" to which a number of works by Mozart or Beethoven were subject. Thus the musical theoretician Jérôme-Joseph Momigny proposed, in his *Cours complet d'harmonie et de composition* published between 1803 and 1806, an "analysis" of the String Quartet in D Minor by Mozart (K. 421), which consisted notably in grafting words (here, a dialogue between Dido and Aeneas) onto the instrumental phrases, in order to explain their metric structure, but also their "true expression."[14] There is in this a kind of modern equivalent of the medieval *trope*, as when they grafted words to certain long melismata (like those in the *Alleluia*), in order to make them easier to memorize, or to make them *clearer*.[15] From a strictly legal point of view, we might speak rather of *adaptations*.

The most famous example of deformation of a work, one related by Berlioz, is undoubtedly that of Castil-Blaze wreaking havoc on Weber's *Freischütz*. In his *Memoirs* (chapter 16), Berlioz speaks of a *Freischütz* that was "mutilated, vulgarized, tortured and insulted in a thousand ways by an arranger," by a "veterinary musician." As Mozart's *Magic Flute* had been, several years previously, when a certain Ludwig Wenceslas Lachnith had produced a French version of it under the title *Les Mystères d'Isis* (1801). Berlioz, despite his indignation, gives a rather exact description of the deformations wrought by Lachnith:

> He stuck *a few bars* on to the end of the overture . . . , turned the soprano part of a chorus into a bass aria, adding a few bars of his own; transplanted the wind instruments from one scene

to another; changed the air and altered the instrumental accompaniment in Sarastro's glorious aria; manufactured a song out of the slaves' chorus, *O cara armonia*; and converted a duet into a trio. (*Memoirs*, 61)

Lengthening, remix, trope, vocal redistribution . . . : all these interventions of the arranger aim at facilitating the communication, that is to say the circulation, of the work in a foreign country, in French opera houses. Berlioz places these deformations on the same level as those performed on theatrical works by translators-adaptors, using an analogy that Liszt, a few years later, would take up and give an entirely different import:

> Mozart was assassinated by Lachnith; Weber, by Castil-Blaze . . . ; Molière and Corneille were cut by unknowns, familiars of the Théâtre-Français; Shakespeare, finally, is still performed in England, in versions by Cibber and some others.[16]

After having been adaptation, *parolisation*, translation (in the weakest sense of a *French version*), after making a past or foreign work conform to the taste of the day in a supposed national culture (like the musical counterpart of what Antoine Berman calls "ethnocentric translation"), arrangement for Berlioz would serve the function of *preservation*: for him it would be a matter, when he becomes an arranger in turn, of *avoiding the worst*. Arrangement ensures a *philological* and *normative* function, as testified by this episode of the *Memoirs*, which we have already read in part, where Berlioz tells why he accepted work on the *Freischütz* (chapter 62):

> The feeling which had urged me to insist on the preservation of Weber's work in its integrity, a feeling which many would call fetishism, *removed all pretext for the manipulations, derangements, suppressions, and corrections, which otherwise would have been eagerly made* (345; emphasis mine).

However, the restorative function of Berlioz's type of arrangement would soon be outflanked, by clashing with the logic it was trying to counter. For, despite all his precautions, Berlioz could not avoid getting caught up in the deforming tendencies in which he had dipped his fingers, though he did so with the best intentions in the world. So we can understand why Berlioz did not want "to be named as author of these recitatives." By refusing to sign, by conferring on his arrangement an essential *museum* function, Berlioz anticipated the decline of this practice, which would accelerate at the end of the nineteenth century. What's more, with phonography, all the so-called communicational functions of arrangement would become moot: no more need to transcribe a symphony for piano so it can be listened to at home . . .

Liszt and the Translators

You will remember that what we had grasped, when listening to Bach-Stokowski, was something else, which didn't have anything to do with the motivations of Stokowski himself when he claimed to be making a practical contribution to the diffusion of Bach, that is to say, to make a replacement for Bach for those who had no access to the organ. This other thing, this strength unique to arrangement that remains when we forget its functions, Liszt found a name for, at least by analogy: he calls it *translation*. But in an entirely different sense, as you will see, from that of adaptations and other French-version *castilblazades*. This word, this fine word "translation," if we read it and listen to it with the attention it deserves, here has quite different resonances from those it had in Berlioz's text. Liszt wrote, in his preface to his transcriptions of Beethoven's symphonies (Rome, 1835): "I will be satisfied if I have accomplished the task of an intelligent engraver, the conscientious translator, who grasps the spirit of a work along with the letter." And again, this time speaking about his piano version of Berlioz's *Symphonie Fantastique*: "I scrupulously tried, *as if it were a matter of translating a sacred text,* to carry over to the piano, not only the musical framework of the symphony, but also the effects and the details."[17]

Indeed, Liszt seems sometimes also to take refuge behind the *public usefulness* of his work, thus denying arrangements all the value peculiar to them: "Arrangements for Piano . . . are not without some advantage, although regarded intrinsically, they are for the most part of mediocre value," he writes in the same preface. And elsewhere (but this is at bottom the flip side of the same idea), he asserts that a bad transcription—a kind of defective copy—while blurring the clean-cut outlines of the original, still fulfills a certain *function*: "The worst lithography," he writes, "the most incorrect translation, still gives a vague idea of the genius of the Michelangelos and Shakespeares."

By thus inscribing arrangement in a series of analogies that confirm in return its devalued status as simple intermediary, Liszt summons up a long tradition, a whole procession of discourses that, from Du Bellay to Montesquieu and beyond (to mention only the French versions), condemns translation as a derivative activity without its own originality. Thus Du Bellay wrote, in the first book of his *Deffense et illustration de la langue françoyse* of 1549: "So he who wishes to produce valuable work in his own vernacular, let him give over this labor of translating, principally the poets, to those who rightly win more modesty than glory from such a laborious and unprofitable, I would even dare to say useless, thing, one even harmful to the development of their language."

Translation, then, has long been contrasted with *making a work* [faire oeuvre]. Longer, in any case, than arrangement, which didn't experience a similar devaluation until much later on: we can find hardly any traces of it before the nineteenth century (which can probably be explained by the history of the notion of the musical work and by the history of copyright, where literature has long preceded music in the construction of authorial values of originality).

Then how should we understand this parallel between arrangement and translation? Is it a simple figure of speech? One that seems just as paradoxical here, placed as it is as an inscription to the wonderful transcriptions by Liszt, as that of the self-effacement found in so many translators' prefaces . . .

We could think, in any case, that this parallel lacks the specificity of music, that it does not take into account its difference from the arts of languages, and that it thus hardly deserves prolonged attention. It might at the very most interest lawyers, who, even today, classify arrangements, adaptations, and translations in the category of *derivative works*—that is to say, derived from the original. But what does it have to say to us today? Didn't Hanslick write, in his famous essay *On the Beautiful in Music*, that music "is a language that we understand and speak, but that is *impossible for us to translate*"?[18] And if, according to Hanslick, the "ideal element" of music is only "sonorous order," if it is never "a notion that *is then translated* by sounds,"[19] what can Liszt's analysis signify, then? The very possibility of translation seems to suppose a distinction between the letter and a meaning that goes beyond it: it is the meaning one translates, the letter remaining forever untranslatable. From then on, supposing that this distinction is lacking in music (especially in so-called "pure" or "absolute" instrumental music), Liszt has produced only a purely superficial comparison.

But that is not the case. And Liszt, despite the quotation from his preface I have just given you to read, makes a definite exception for arrangers, when they set out to talk about their "labor." That is why this musician of musicians, as much by his discourse as by his work on the music of others, will lead us to understand our listenings differently. For, even if we grant Hanslick his formalistic presuppositions before the term was invented (his essay was written in 1854), even if we think that the "meaning" of music is musical through and through—thus that it cannot be separated from its letter—the fact is that thinking about arrangement by way of the mirror of translation opens up beautiful perspectives to us listeners. That is what I would like to convince you of.

I have said that I love arrangers; and it's probably for the same reasons that I love translators. I always have the impression, in fact, of reading them in the process of reading, of *reading their reading* of a work. They sign their reading just as arrangers sign their listening. And that is why every reflection on reading—on what it is to *read a text*—should include the question of translation.[20] That is also why arrangers have so many things to tell us about our listening to a work. About what listening means; and about what we can understand by the *work*. Literally.

Before I return to Liszt—before we continue reading his preface and listening to him at his trade, in the process of writing down his hearing of the Beethoven symphonies—a few words, then on translators. And on their long history as a story of suspense.

The Original in Suspense

After Du Bellay, it is still the same process that is seemingly depicted by Montesquieu in 1721, in this dialogue in the *Persian Letters* between a geometrician and a translator;[21] the latter says to the former:

"I have a great piece of news to tell you: I have just presented my Horace to the public." "What!" the geometrician said, "he lived two thousand years ago." "You don't understand me," the other continued: "It is a translation of that ancient author that I have just given birth to; I have spent twenty years on the translations." "What! Sir," the geometrician said, "it's been twenty years since you last thought anything? You speak for others, and they think for you? . . . I have as much respect as anyone else for the sublime geniuses that you have within you.

But you don't resemble them in the least: for, if you always translate, others will never translate you. . . . You want, you say, to make these illustrious dead live again among us, and I confess that you do indeed give them a body; but you do not give them back their life: a spirit to animate them is always lacking."

If I briefly evoke a few of these attacks on translators, if I amplify the implicit resonances with which Liszt composes when he inscribes arrangement next to translation, it is in order to outline the progression of the line, the connecting thread that will accompany us when I question the practice of arrangement. This thread—which we have to follow, I think, to understand something about our listenings—is stretched, so to speak, between two opposite polarizations of one single idea, which is expressed in a way by the geometrician in the *Persian Letters*: *if you always translate, others will never translate you.* It is in fact this same saying that we find, with a change of polarity, in the discourse on translation that has perhaps given rise to the most commentaries: that of Walter Benjamin in "The Task of the Translator." This is a major text that completely revolutionizes our thinking about translation, if at least we understand it in a certain way.

Benjamin writes:

The higher the level of a work, the more does it remain translatable even if its meaning is touched upon only fleetingly. This, of course, applies to originals only. *Translations, on the other hand, prove to be untranslatable* not because of any inherent difficulty, but because of the looseness with which meaning attaches to them.[22] (emphasis mine)

Here we find Montesquieu's geometrician's formula, but strangely shifted: translation is in effect untranslatable (people do not translate translators), but now this is no longer so, as in

The Persian Letters, because it lacks "spirit"; on the contrary, one could say, paraphrasing Benjamin, it is untranslatable because at bottom, in relation to an original that is full of meaning, it reveals that, already in this original, the "meaning" or the "spirit" is not the essential thing. Translation, then, is nothing more than "body," almost. Because it has only a particularly fleeting relationship with "meaning" (with the "spirit"). And, precisely, that is not its weakness, but rather its own strength.

Let's try to understand this singular strength of translation, so that later on, we can approach the strength of arrangement.

Benjamin writes:

> No translation would be possible if in its ultimate essence it strove for likeness to the original. For in its afterlife—which could not be called that if it were not a transformation and a renewal of something living—the original undergoes a change. Even words with fixed meaning can undergo a maturing process. (73)

In other words, translation is possible only because the original needs to be transformed in order to survive. In an "afterlife" worthy of that name. And Benjamin stresses that this transformation or deformation, this *plasticity* of the original, is not due to the arbitrary nature or "subjectivity" of one translator or another; it is not the skill or awkwardness of translators that causes the original to be distorted, but rather "the very life of language and its works" (73). The original is plastic because it is *made of language*. And because this language *lives*. From then on, translation is not a "sterile equation of two dead languages"; on the contrary, it is the sign of "the maturing process of the original language."

If, in fact, the original survives in a language that continues to live, by that very fact it becomes foreign to its own language: think of a text written in "Old French" . . . But this becoming-foreign of the original does not wait for centuries: it affects its language from the beginning. Benjamin does not indeed express it that way, but his text calls for this reading: namely, that the original, in order to survive and by surviving, demands to be translated into its "own" language become "alien." And, after that, translation only reveals an essential instability of the original, notably in what it "intends" (76).

Benjamin seems to say that the "intention"—that is to say, if you like, the "meaning" or the "spirit"—is not already there in the original: it is rather somewhere on the horizon, at the (endless) end of its afterlife in languages. At the endless end of its translations:

> In the individual, unsupplemented languages, meaning is never found in relative independence . . . ; rather, it is in a constant state of flux—until it is able to emerge as pure language from the harmony of all the various modes of intention. Until then, it remains hidden in the languages. (74)

Translation does not aim for meaning, then, since meaning is waiting, *in suspense* [en souffrance], endlessly deferred; it cannot aim for what it must, on the contrary, *leave to be desired*. In a translation, unlike in the original, the letter does not in essence refer to a meaning; it is rather a relationship *of language to language*. And it is here that Benjamin radically shifts the notion of translation; for if, for him as well as for so many others, the translator has *nothing of his own to say*, that is precisely his strength, the originality of his "labor." He is not uttering something, he is not moved by a *meaning-to-say* [vouloir-dire]; he speaks about languages [*il parle des langues*, also meaning "he speaks various languages"], he is conveying something of the relationship among several languages. And in that, positively, he *leaves something to be desired*. Because, for Benjamin, translation "is only a somewhat provisional way of coming to terms with the foreignness of languages" (75).

That is why, moreover, good translation, according to Benjamin, must not erase the resistance of the letter to make way for meaning; it should not *substitute* for the original, but on the contrary let it be desired in the strangeness of its language:

> The greatest praise one can make of a translation is not that it reads as if it had originally been written in that language. Rather, the significance of fidelity as ensured by literalness is that, from the work [*aus dem Werke*], the great longing [*Sehnsucht*] for linguistic complementation [*Sprachergänzung*] can speak. A real translation is transparent; it does not cover the original. (79 [translation modified])

Transparency, according to Benjamin, has nothing to do, then, with the "readability" of a translation, with its ease of reading. It is rather what, in it, *leaves to be desired* by making the reader pause.

What is to be desired?

Incompleteness, fragmentation: that of translation, but also that of the original, inasmuch as both *summon* the complementarity of the other language. Benjamin in fact says that "in all language and linguistic creations," there remains "something that cannot be communicated" (79). The incommunicable that is at issue here is obviously not meaning. In the case of the original, this incommunicable is the "symbolizing" (79). That is, in another vocabulary, the signifier, the letter. The literality of the original is thus its incommunicable. Now, "in the evolving of languages," that is, *in the movement of translation*, this incommunicable becomes the "symbolized." In other words, what translation signifies or represents, what it makes a *sign* toward in any case, is this literality of the original. Which can be read or understood only *from* its translation. It is this translation that lets the original be desired as "pure language," that is to say, as *pure literality*. Translation is not the restoration of the original;

it expresses on the contrary its *literal pending nature* [la souf-france à la lettre], by tearing it away from its fastening or moor-ing, from the weightiness of its meaning. It is up to translation, according to Benjamin, to "extract" this literal "ultimate es-sence" from meaning to express it:

> To turn the symbolizing into the symbolized . . . is the tremen-dous and only capacity of translation. In this pure language—which no longer means or expresses anything . . . —all information, all sense, and all intention finally encounter a stratum in which they are destined to be extinguished. (80)

By making a kind of sacred text that is no longer intent on communicating something, translation, and it alone, "symbol-izes" the letter of the original. It signifies it, represents it, or says it literally. That is why, faced with the original, *translation is the letter of its letter.*

In the remarkable reading he gave of "The Task of the Transla-tor," Paul de Man—especially when he comments on the passage about which I emphasized a change of polarity of the phrasing in the *Persian Letters*—says almost the same thing:

> In a strange way, translation canonizes its own version, mak-ing it more canonical than the original was. That the original was not purely canonical is obvious from the fact that it re-quires translation: it could not be definitive since it can be translated. But, says Benjamin, you cannot translate a transla-tion. . . . You can translate only an original. Translation canon-izes, fixes an original, while demonstrating a mobility in it, an instability that one had not immediately noticed.[23]

Thus, the original would not have been the original (in the canonical or sacred sense of the word) without translation, which it summons. The original, in order to be what it literally is, is in need of translation. But, on the other hand, it is *mobilized*, forced to let this instability that was its own become understood. The original gives itself to the letter only through the translation that opens it up and carries it away.

Arrangement at Work (Liszt, Second Version)

Benjamin doesn't say a word about music—that is not his intention—although certain metaphors in his text seem to evoke it.[24] However, our reading continues to be magnetized, subliminally, by musical listening. And by this *writing down of listening* that is arrangement. So it is time to take Liszt's analogy seriously; to take it at its word, literally, rather than as a simple metaphor.

Let us listen to Liszt, let us listen to his arrangements from the immense perspective opened up by Benjamin.

With one hand, I open the orchestral score of the fourth movement ("The Tempest" [of Beethoven's *Pastoral* Symphony]). And, with the other, I open the piano transcription of it written by Liszt.

In Liszt, I come first of all, without even looking at the notes, upon a mass of instrumental indications: *Tutti,* "bassoon," "clarinet" . . . In these names of instruments destined *for the pianist alone,* the absent orchestra is *noted* everywhere.

We could think that these words are put there as dynamic or articulatory indications; they might in a way be synonyms, intended for the pianist, for *piano, staccato, dolce,* and so on . . . *Tutti* might mean *fortissimo,* "clarinet" might mean *legato*; in one case, you would have to play with the cumulative power of the entire orchestra and, in the other, link the notes together as a wind instrument would do in one single breath. But the usual notations (*fortissimo,* slurs . . .) are *also* present. They are, so to speak, *redoubled* by the names of the absent instruments. If they *specify* a nuance or a phrasing, if they *give shape* (and we will see what kind of shape) to more abstract indications, that would not be the only reason for these inscriptions.

Nor are these inscriptions a *function* similar to the one they could have in the piano reduction of an opera. A reduction is in effect mainly destined for a practical use, for example to help singers rehearse without using the entire orchestra every time; and so we can understand why, for the very reason of its function, it must include the exact identification of one solo instrument or another preparing the way for the singing voice, or the voice conversing with it. There is nothing like that here, in what we should rather describe as a *transcription* (a word that, as we will see, Liszt implicitly contrasts with arrangement or reduction). What's more, in a letter to a certain Adolphe Pictet[25]— which foreshadows the very words of the preface that we have begun to read—Liszt goes even further; speaking of his very first transcription, that of Berlioz's *Symphonie Fantastique*, he writes, "I gave my work the title of *Piano Score* [*Partition de piano*] in order to make more obvious the intention to follow the orchestra step by step."

By baptizing his transcription "piano score" (instead of *score for* piano), Liszt implicitly removes it from any kind of utilitarian perspective; moreover, his title, whose importance he himself stresses, obviously evokes what we currently call an orchestral score [*une partition d'orchestre*]. His "partition *de* piano" is thus a kind of orchestral score *on the piano*. That is why, in the *Pastoral* Symphony as well as in the *Fantastique* that preceded it, the names are signs of absence; they imply the inscription of the absence of or desire for the original in the hollow of the transcription. They literally create longing (*Sehnsucht*, "yearning," Benjamin would say) for its many instruments.

But they also say something about the subject of the pianist himself who is about to interpret them. They are like a question aimed at him. Alfred Brendel, in a text devoted to Liszt's arrangements and paraphrases,[26] wondered: "How can one reproduce the timbre of other instruments on the piano?" That is indeed what the names of the absent instruments seem to ask here.

Brendel's answer says a lot about the *plasticity* of a body summoned to interpret the lack: "I get the sound of the oboe"—the sound that Liszt seems to ask for by indicating *Ob.* at measure 19—"by rounding out and curling up my fingers (which almost makes the bones stick out) and by playing *poco legato*." The instrumental and interpretative body lets itself be shaped here by the wish to be these absent sonorous bodies.

The body that shapes transcription is thus *plastic*. As is also (I had suggested this about Bach-Stokowski) our listening to an arrangement, torn between two parallel lines, one present and the other ghostly or spectral: our listening is stretched, stretched to breaking point like a rubber band, between the transcription and the original. That is to say, here, in Liszt, between the piano score and the orchestral score.

This tension is present in every arrangement, even the most simplistic or the kitschiest. But the remarkable thing about Liszt's transcription, what makes it unique in the vast corpus of arrangements in general, is that it continually *notes, in its very wording*, this state of lability or instability. Thus, in certain measures of his transcription of the *Pastoral* Symphony,[27] Liszt gives, one over the other, *two possible versions* for the corresponding orchestral passage. *Ossia*, we read on the score: an Italian term ("also") that, in Liszt's time, usually designated the existence of a less difficult instrumental way to perform the piece (the term is used often in pedagogical works). But Liszt's *ossia* is inexplicable here in exclusively *technical* terms, just on the level of interpretation and its difficulties. The second version is technically *more difficult*; and moreover, when the *same* orchestral passage returns later on *identically*, Liszt no longer uses the *ossia* and keeps only *the most difficult* of the two versions.[28]

So we must look for the reason for these variations elsewhere than in pianistic technique: once again, as for the dynamic and instrumental indications, the coexistence of two competing versions cannot be explained in terms of *function*. *Ossia*, taken literally, is *useless*.

It would seem rather that, faced with an orchestral complexity that is materially *irreducible* to the piano and to two hands,[29] faced with a physical or surgical limit, Liszt has in a way *compensated for the impossible by multiplying the possibilities*. The symphonic original being here more distant or more absent than ever, Liszt tries to let it be heard (or let it be desired) *between the lines of his versions*. I do not know of any other example of a transcriber knowingly giving *several simultaneous versions* of his original: by this writing down of a plural listening, Liszt becomes an exception among arrangers.

As to his discourse (his preface and his letters), he indeed often engages in the classic process of functionalization and devaluation, in the lineage of traditional concepts of arrangement or translation. However, the preface, at second glance, reverses the previous process. And it does so by seemingly changing the subject, by no longer talking about arrangement itself, but about the arranger's instrument, namely the piano: "But," writes Liszt, "the extension acquired by the Piano in recent times, due to progress in performance and the perfecting of the mechanism, allows us to do more, better than had been done before now." In other words, it is indeed a mutation of *bodies*—of the instrumental body as well as the interpretative body—that opens new possibilities to translate music to the letter:

> By the unlimited development of its harmonic power, the Piano tends more and more to assimilate to itself all orchestral compositions. In the space of its seven octaves, it can produce, with few exceptions, all the features, all the combinations . . . and leaves to the orchestra no other superiorities (although these are, it is true, immense) than those of the diversity of timbres and the effects of the massed forces.

With the progress of organology, Liszt has thus been able to *translate* the *Pastoral*. Or rather to incorporate it, *to appropriate it into its own body*, while still giving it a tension, an elasticity that it had never had before. Liszt, to use Paul de Man's phrase, did indeed "canonize" the *Pastoral*, but he did this by revealing in it, with his *ossia*, an unsuspected mobility. It is this instability of the work that I would like to preserve always by having you listen to my listenings: in order to *let you desire* the pure language of a symphony that, before us, before *both* of us, was never heard *literally*.

But this *strict appropriation* is possible only *from* the transcription conceived as the transfer and reinscription of the music in *another body*. The experience or ordeal of the work's tension (an entirely different thing from its simple presence) is at play here in this coming-and-going: between a letter and the body that it becomes *via a foreign body*. This can be, as it is here, the knowing and virtuoso body of the pianist; but this can also be, as you will see, *our body*, as soon as it is fitted out with the *instruments of listening* that are our phonographic prostheses.

Schumann the Critic

By following Liszt *at work*, have we broken away from a substitutive (because functional) concept of arrangement? Have we broken our face-to-face confrontation with the work? I think that we have *triangulated* it. Between Beethoven and me there is Liszt the listener, reinscribing his listenings for the piano. And I *listen to him listening*.

Similarly, between my selected extracts and you, I am there. With my machines, with my listener's instruments prolonging my ears, with my body *equipped*. And, *from you to me*, we begin now to turn the work and its listening into an experience. To hear hearing: it is from this reduplication that something like a *critical moment* of listening arises.

Schumann, to whom I turn now, seems to have perceived this, in his own way.

Schumann was also a music critic (he founded the *Neue Zeitschrift für Musik*, of which he became the sole editor and owner in 1835). In December 1833, an article he published in the literary journal *Kommet* explicitly linked music criticism to the idea of the *perfectibility* of works: "The critic should hide nothing!" he wrote; "all artistic attempts are approximate; there is no work of art that is not capable of being improved."[30]

Schumann seems to suggest thus that a work is not given immediately in all its completeness: but that on the contrary it awaits, it summons, criticism (and I will add: arrangement). In this he may go even further than Liszt, to whom he always paid the warmest tribute by lauding the piano version of Berlioz's *Symphonie Fantastique*: "Liszt worked on this reduction with so much ardor and enthusiasm that it should be considered an original work. . . . In these conditions, the reduction for piano can be heard boldly alongside the orchestral performance itself."[31]

Arrangement here becomes an "original work," which still does not impose itself *in place of* the original, but can be heard *alongside* it. The status of arrangement that is thus outlined is difficult to label: it is that of a work, indeed, but one that seems destined to run alongside the other, its model. To follow it without being subordinate to it, but also without being completely detached from it: a kind of *alliance*, like a shadow that, while still remaining linked to the body whose silhouette it is, has acquired a certain autonomy in its movements.

It is this strange shadow that interests me: it is this that can lead us toward a certain Romantic concept of arrangement, in the strong sense of *music criticism in music.*

That arrangement (transcribing, writing *based on* . . .) disturbs and questions the work (of the arranged as well as of the arranger) is what Schumann could suggest better than any other on the subject of his "own" *Six Concert Etudes After Paganini Caprices* (op. 10); he writes, in 1836: "I am giving an opus number [*eine Opuszahl*] to these etudes, because the publisher told me they would make their way better that way . . . a reason that made all my objections fall away."[32] Schumann did not want to regard his *Six Etudes* as a work "composed *after*." He objected, he says, to seeing them counted as an *opus*, but ended up deferring to his publisher's arguments. But, while crediting it to his work, this editorial comment *notes*, discreetly and almost secretly (like a cipher or a code), the undecidability of its status. We don't really know how to attribute the operation to which Schumann gives himself over here "based on" Paganini; we can only attribute it to an "unknown greatness": "But in silence," Schumann continues, "I looked at the X [the opus number 10 that has now become a Roman numeral and a capital letter] as the sign of the unknown greatness (the *x*) and the composition . . . as authentically Paganinian [*eine echte Paganinische*]."

Everything is at stake here in the capital letter, in the shift to capital, in *capitalization*. When the number 10 is changed into the letter X, it gains in greatness (majesty of the majuscule) as well as in its indeterminacy, in a particularly dense context rich in implicit allusions. What is at stake here?

Schumann, in a parenthesis we should reread, had written precisely this: "But in silence I looked at the number X (for I am not yet at the ninth muse) as the sign of unknown greatness (the *x*)." This parenthesis is complex, in its allusive overdetermination. It is of capital importance for the way it implies a Romantic concept of arrangement; so we should linger over it a little.

The Muses, daughters of Zeus, are, we know, nine in number: they traditionally represent the division of the "liberal arts" into nine figures, under the protection of Apollo (called "Musagetes," Leader of the Muses). Now Schumann has projected this division and difference in the arts (and he is not alone in doing so; Wagner will do it also) onto the nine symphonies of Beethoven. This he has done in 1836, the very year of the publication of the article on the *Six Etudes*, op. X, in the *Neue Zeitschrift für Musik*. In this "Monument to the Glory of Beethoven," Schumann writes:

> If I were a prince, I would build him a temple in the style of Palladio: there would be ten statues there. . . . I want nine statues along with his own, the number of the Muses, since that is also the number of his symphonies: Cleo would represent the *Heroica*, Thalia the *Fourth*, Euterpe the *Pastorale*, and so on, and he himself would be the divine Musagetes.

If, according to a process that Schumann only outlines here (and that Wagner would later systematize in *The Art-Work of the Future*), each of Beethoven's symphonies can be associated with one of the arts, the number X is charged with resonances that, for readers of Schumann, could not not be heard. How can we not see in it, in fact, the echo of an unknown, dreamt-of post-Ninth? How can we not see lurking, between these discreet lines of Schumann's on his arrangement "based on" Paganini, the ghost of an impossible *Tenth*, as if forbidden in advance (and made all the more desirable) by the famous *Ninth* that, by opening the instrumental symphony to language and to the singing voice, also opened up musical Romanticism as such?

The *post-Ninth* (IX + I) was the impossible and endlessly unfinished task of this musical Romanticism. (Think of, among so many others, Mahler, who would leave his Tenth in a fragmented state . . .). By making the *words* of Schiller's language enter the sphere of so-called "pure" music, Beethoven's *Ninth* and its final ode to joy undermined a certain difference in the arts and a certain distinction of genres. What would come afterwards was the unknown: the x, small or great.

For Wagner, this would be the monumental work uniting all the arts; it would be the *Gesamtkunstwerk* or "total art-work" (as the accepted translation expresses it) that would come to replace the seemingly unsurpassable compositional summit of the "last symphony."[33] But for Schumann—the musician who, more than any other, grasped a certain *fragmentary requirement* stemming from the first literary Romanticism (that of Jena and the *Athenaeum*)—this x seems to signify something entirely different from a monumental replacement. For Schumann, who was also a music critic, the post-Ninth unknown could be a new relationship with works and with time: a relationship *based on*. A "minor" relationship, a relationship *of arrangement*. For Schumann (at least in this context, all of whose consequences he surely did not grasp), arrangement is the "unknown greatness" coming to rest in the space between the work and the Work: an essentially *critical* space, if it is true that it is the task of criticism to try to complete the movement of the work toward its Idea.

What Schumann registers here, in these paragraphs devoted to a minor work (as arrangement always is, faced with uppercase Music), is the *strong* Romantic sense of arrangement: the sense that sets arrangement alongside the *ideal work* and the impossible (the Work). Remote from its (too obvious) function of dissemination (before the days of recording), a certain Romantic arrangement can be heard only from the abyss between the work and the Work. By noting the distance that always keeps the work just short of the Work, arrangement posits the Work as an ideal that remains still to be unveiled or developed *beyond* the work. As its Idea. That is how Schumann can explain that, in his op. X, he sought something completely different from his previous op. 3 (which also gathered together *Etudes for the Piano Based on Paganini's Violin Caprices*):

> I had, perhaps to its detriment, copied the original almost note for note, and limited myself to completing it from the harmonic standpoint, except that this time I set aside the pedantry of a textual transcription, and wanted the present transcription [the op. X] to give the impression of an autonomous piano composition, which would make one forget its violin origin, without the work losing any of its *poetic Idea*. (234; emphasis mine)

In other words, by this strange operation of "Schumann" (whose nature as a work remains and must remain *unknown*, despite all the editorial remarks that try to attest to it), the arranger this time intends opus X to be able to extract, from all its original contingencies, something like the Work and its Idea. By aiming for the *Idea behind the letter*, Schumann continues, *tries to complete the movement of the work toward the Work* that Paganini had only outlined:

Paganini himself must make his talent as a composer ring out louder than his eminent genius as virtuoso. Although one can also, at least in the present day, not be wholly in agreement with him on this, there appears, in his compositions, especially in the violin caprices . . . so many diamonds that the richest ornamentation demanded by the piano could only strengthen them, far from making them fade away. (234)

Arrangement, according to (or *after* Schumann), is thus *a critique of music in music.* In the precise sense that Friedrich Schlegel had in mind when he wrote in the *Athenaeum,* "Poetry can be critiqued only by poetry. A judgment about art that is not itself a work of art . . . has no validity in the realm of art." Like literary criticism, like translation too, as they were thought of in early Jena romanticism,[34] arrangement according to Schumann aims for the completion of the work toward (in) the Work, according to an infinite process that is that of the Idea. And it is essential that this criticism not only remain undecidable in its "own" status as work (as *opus*), but that it also disturb the established distinction of artistic genres (especially the border between music and language).

Decline of Arrangement (Why Is Music So Hard to Understand?)

It is starting from *this* heritage of Romanticism that we can begin to think about such a thing as *active, critical listening.* It is in this space, so opened, that I dream of hearing us listen.

But a certain historical paradox has willed it that, at the very moment when this heritage was explicitly recognized, at the very moment when the practice of arrangement had elevated status conferred on it, its outlines were confused to the point of blurring, dissolving, erasing its identity and its "own" strength. Ferruccio Busoni, composer and virtuoso pianist, (self-)proclaimed heir of Liszt, is both one of the great craftsmen and the symptom of this transformation in which the *decline of arrangement* began in the very moment of its glory.

In a text symbolically entitled "The Value of Arrangement,"[35] published in Berlin in November 1910, Busoni seems in fact to recognize arrangement as having an important and legitimate status; but he does so only by driving it back to *composition*, that is to say by minimizing, even by denying its tension vis-à-vis an actual work:

> I came to think that *every notation is already the transcription of an abstract invention*. From the instant the pen takes hold of it, the idea loses its original feature. . . . The invention [*Einfall*] becomes a sonata, or a concerto: it is already an arrangement of the original. From this first transcription to the second, the step is, by comparison, minimal and insignificant. In general, however, it is only to the second that great importance is attached. And we lose sight, after that, of the fact that a transcription does not destroy the original version, thus that there is no degradation. . . . *For the musical work of art exists before having sounded and after it has resounded, it is there complete and intact. It is both in time and outside of time.*

By making the musical work into something timeless, an Idea that is somehow embodied in time, as if only intermittently, Busoni forbids in advance the gesture that constituted the "unique" strength of arrangement. For the Idea, here, *precedes* the work; and from then on, if arrangement seems to raise itself to the rank of composition, this is simply because it shares its imperfection, its *original sin*. This perspective is entirely different from the one we can imagine after Schumann and a certain Liszt. The difference, seemingly minimal and yet abyssal, goes from the *original defect* to the *defect of origin*. On one hand, in Busoni, the Idea is a prerequisite that notation (composing or arranging) can grasp only imperfectly. And, on the other, it *remains forever yet to come*, receding to the horizon, at the endless end of arrangements and rewritings that reserve the possibility of its *survival. Nach-leben* [literally, "to live after"], said Benjamin—a German word whose *active* sense the English "survive" conveys poorly.

Paradoxically, there is in Busoni, in this text that is probably the greatest hymn ever written to the glory of arrangers, a fore-shadowing of the decline of this activity, one that would become more and more secondary, if not impossible. At least in the framework of a Western tradition that has been called "schol-arly." It is this movement of decline, this atrophy, that continues in Schoenberg, who countered with the firmest rejection possible of the arrangement Busoni offered him of his piece for piano, op. 11, no. 2.[36]

As Adorno wrote:

> When Busoni . . . eagerly seized on a piece for piano by Schoenberg (op. 11, no. 2), he ended up with a virtuoso carica-ture; not only, as a common argument that is too easily pleased with progress would have it, because "we are still too close to Schoenberg," not only because the "concertante inter-pretation" by Busoni in fact considerably lacks fidelity to the text; but because this piece for the piano fully preserves only what Schoenberg himself wanted to say; because it thus con-firms in such a suitable way that it does not tolerate, out of principle, interpretative liberty, not to mention the arbitrari-ness of an arranger. Neither today, nor later on.[37]

As soon as arrangement is no longer the equation by which the work = X, either it offers itself in respect for the original, or it is on the side of composition pure and simple. In both cases, its critical force is lost; we are alone, in a confrontation with works that fulfill *the other* great Romantic impulse that musical modernity has inherited (precisely by blocking out the former, by closing up the space of an operative plasticity): we touch the ultimate point of an affirmation of the values of authenticity and authorship. And it is at that exact moment that Music, endowed with a capital letter that has nothing uncertain about it, becomes "hard to understand."

"Why Is Schoenberg's Music So Hard to Understand?" is the title of an article published by Alban Berg in 1924.[38] As for the diagnosis that this title pronounces (and that the article explains by justifying it), at bottom nothing has changed (or so little has). We have only to read the recent statements of a musician like Steve Reich: "The mailman will *never* whistle Schoenberg. . . . His music (and all music that resembles his) will always inhabit a kind of 'dark little corner,' isolated from the history of all the music in the World."[39]

But it is perhaps not so much a question of "understanding" Schoenberg (which would come down, as a prejudice still widely held today has it, to deciding whether or not his music has a "meaning"); it is a question of whether or not one is able to *appropriate* it. We have, then, to *translate* Schoenberg: not in the sense of making him legible, of acclimating his language to a supposedly more familiar language; but in Benjamin's sense of translation, that of opening up a space of complementarity (better: of *tension*) among *several* languages. And perhaps we even have to take listening to his music (to *the* music) away from any horizon ruled by an analogy with language, in order to think of it rather, along with a certain Liszt, as the plastic play of several bodies.

In other words, it is a question of *sending* it, from me to you, in a movement that is not that of hermeneutic comprehension, or that of a virtuous offering; but that of a *reinscription in bodies*. Which supposes that we others, who do not play the piano (or who seldom play it), can learn, with our phonographic listening instruments, to be equal to the authentic task of translators. Better: transducers.

CHAPTER 3 *Our Instruments for Listening Before the Law (Second Journal Entry)*

I've just finished listening to you know what, by you know who. On a disk. I raised the volume right at the part you know. Very loud, just to see the result. All the rest, what there is before and after that moment, has become like a backdrop from which our passage stood out with a contrast that I had never heard in it before. Modestly, with the feeling of having in my hands a blunt, rough chisel, I couldn't rid myself of the haunting idea that I was the conductor of what I was hearing: my tools—that ridiculous volume knob called a potentiometer—were the coarsest possible, but I was still master of a certain *articulation of my listening.*

For an instant I dreamed of what this passage would become when slowed down. I thought of W., that time when we had gotten it into our heads to decipher Charlie Parker's solos. With his equipment (an old tape recorder), we could slow down the speed of these rockets of notes that seemed to us like curtains hiding a treasure of invention. Obviously, by changing the speed, we made Parker more serious. The Bird lost his wings. And if we stretched it out, if we slowed it down more and more, in our desire to hear it *under a magnifying glass*, Bird left the melodic realm of the song, and let only muffled notes be heard, as if struck under water. He had changed, he had become a croaking animal.

What we were doing then, with W., to observe Bird's phrasing as if under the microscope in order to reproduce all its nuances and all its *tricks*, is what almost all jazz musicians have done. Parker himself learned how to improvise with a phonograph on which he replayed the riffs of Lester Young and a few others.[1] But that wasn't *in order to listen*, you'll say to me: that was with the purpose of appropriating others' music, in order to integrate it into his own improvisations. Of course you are right, there is a real difference of perspective there distinguishing him from us simple listeners.

After that for a long time I stopped, as you know, deciphering Bird's improvisations. In any case, you can find them published now, transcribed note by note, by expert, well-equipped listeners, who proceed no differently than we did. Armed with tape recorders or record players, they examine under the microscope and restore in their slightest inflections lightning-quick licks.

Some people, however, use this set of tools that we have, these changes in volume and speed, for completely other reasons than faithful, literal transcription. I think of those DJs we went to listen to the other day. They are indeed musicians—there was even a poster, a program, we paid for our seat to attend a concert . . . And yet, all they did in front of us—with a confounding virtuosity—was at bottom nothing more than the gestures I perform for you, in private, in the comfort of a living room: I adjust the volume, I jump from track to track, I blend or mix two disks, I slow them down or speed them up. . . .

Speaking of us, of our disks, Walter Benjamin wrote: "The cathedral leaves its locale to be received in the studio of a lover of art; the choral production, performed in an auditorium or in the open air, resounds in the drawing room."[2] In short, with what he called "the era of [its] mechanical reproduction," music, taken away from the here and now of the concert, came into our homes: it became available everywhere and at any instant, anywhere and anytime. You could bring it home or take it on a trip. You could bring Charlie Parker or Lester Young home, either simply to listen to them again or, as Bartók said, to observe in slow motion, "as if we were analyzing an object under the magnifying glass," the "minute characteristics of interpretation."[3]

But it seems to me that with our DJs another era of listening may be beginning, which I don't know what to call. It is no longer that of the aforementioned mechanical reproduction, but rather one where production, reproduction, and reception tend to be *confused*. Not so much to become equivalent as to share the same gestures and the same instruments. For if the DJs are essentially doing nothing different from what I do in my listening room, that is because they are simply *listeners appearing in concert*. I am not the only one to think this; it was a musician who recently said, speaking of them, that their art "implies less a knowledge of how to play than of a knowledge of how to listen."[4]

You know, I think we have to face facts: we listeners have *instruments*. When I speak to you about my fascination with these new *auditory magnifying glasses*, it is not an image: it is the truth of our listenings, naked as perhaps it has never been before. And I often wonder what they would have thought of all this equipment, our Zachariases and our Tyszkiewiczes. What would they have said when they saw my new acquisition, which allows me not only to jump from track to track to go directly to my chosen extracts, but also to superimpose two disks, to record what I want onto a third, to inscribe my bookmarks or my *track-marks*, to lower or raise the volume, to take away the bass or the treble, to add echo effects (my favorite being precisely the cathedral)? Perhaps Zacharias, the older of the two, would have enthusiastically multiplied the footnotes. While the other would have needed a whole firm of lawyers working day and night . . .

I'm serious, you know I am. We listeners have become arrangers. Adorno understood this, writing in 1938, "The sonorous modifications that every orchestra undergoes when it resounds in a room through loudspeakers are themselves a kind of arrangement."[5] Which is a completely different thing, I think, from mechanical reproduction. And that is indeed the problem. *Our* problem. For, you'll remember, in the vast historical trial we have inherited, the devaluation of arrangement tended to lower it to the rank of a bad copy equal to a counterfeit. (And even Adorno, with all his intuition, did not think otherwise, I think.)

What do we have the right to do, then, with all the *instruments for listening* that we have at our disposal? Whatever we like, you'll tell me, so long as we stay home, so long as our listenings do not leave the reserved sphere of our private life, which is no one's business. Indeed, I grant you that; no actual law—and this is fortunate—regulates our domestic listenings, even the wildest ones. But that doesn't prevent our listenings from being paralyzed by laws in a more subliminal way. The strange Count Tyszkiewicz has shown us by his exemplary example: with time, listeners are permeable to legal precedents that locate musical works in the field of commerce; they drink them and absorb them—often without realizing it—to the point of sometimes themselves transforming into judges. That is why I continue the journal of our ancestors, I pursue the archaeology of our rights through the discourse of the courts on our instruments for listening.

The First Trial of Mechanical Music (Verdi on the Boards)

Tito Ricordi was Verdi's publisher in Italy. Ricordi—whose name aptly evokes recording—gave a speech full of scorn for "traveling musicians" and their "street organs" in front of the august assembly of the first international congress on copyright laws that took place in Brussels in 1858:

> It often happens that the finest thoughts of certain operas that have not yet been performed in a city receive publicity in advance by means of traveling musicians and street organs [i.e., barrel organs]: usually they are reproduced with all sorts of cuts, with horrible alterations of harmony and inflections, with arrangements that are so bad, that not only does the music lose its lyrical, dramatic, and vocal characteristic, but also the melodies themselves undergo the strangest metamorphoses. —The first impression of this music on the public has all the impression of *monotony* [emphasis mine: in other

words, *mechanicity*], of discordance, of vulgarity; the public is sated and disgusted with it in advance; to the point that, when it comes later on to hear the original performance, what is new seems old to it, the beautiful seems ugly, spontaneity is now just a triviality.[6]

Ricordi gives voice, here, to some of the most recurrent *topoi* about reproductive instruments: their vulgarity, the indifference they generate. But, beyond these commonplaces, what matters to us listeners is the *linked* denigration of arrangement and of the mechanization of music. For Ricordi's speech was not an isolated fact: we have to suspect a systematic link between, on one hand, the reproducible setting of music and, on the other, arrangement conceived in a restrictive way as a counterfeit substituting itself for the work. And it is precisely in these same years that the courts would be confronted with new questions raised by the development and distribution of mechanical musical instruments.

Starting from the hydraulic organs of Antiquity, these instruments have had a long history.[7] And some were swiftly associated with archival properties. Thus, in 1775, in a treatise devoted to the art of making musical cylinders,[8] a certain Engramelle (whose name again evokes the gramophone) regretted that the music of "Lulli, Marchand, & all the great men" was not transmitted "by themselves to posterity on some inalterable cylinders." Engramelle used the term *notage* to designate the way "to calculate Music; to measure its notes by numbers, & to divide the circumference of cylinders into so many equal parts, which one might need, in order to apply prongs to them at precise distances, & to arrange them there in a way to perform with taste & precision the pieces of Music one wants to have played by machines."

With their serrated cylinder that causes metal strips to sound, most music boxes were made that way, ones that I sometimes amuse myself by winding up for you: instruments that I readily associate with childhood, reproducing nursery rhymes to the sound of which one falls asleep; instruments evoking naiveté, innocence . . . Never would I have suspected that they could in turn give birth to apparatuses that would end up in court, accused of the worst crimes against music.

In 1846, the instrument maker Alexandre François Debain filed a patent for his invention of the *antiphonal* [antiphonel]. When you cranked it up, this instrument, which used "small boards" [*planchettes*] pricked with nails rather than cylinders, made the keys of a keyboard play. Destined first for the organ, it was soon adapted for the piano, giving birth to the *Pianista Debain*. This quickly had an immense success, and Debain began to sell "boards" reproducing all kinds of melodies in fashion. Among the most requested, ranking high up in the "hit parade," were airs from Verdi's *I vespri siciliani*, the French rights to which belonged to the Escudier brothers. They had a bailiff seize the "boards" of *I vespri* in Debain's studio, along with other titles to which they had exclusive rights. In the trial that ensued, Louis Nouguier, the lawyer for the publisher plaintiffs, explained first that, although the musical machines in question had already existed for a long time, it was the popularity that the industry had recently enjoyed that now motivated recourse to the law:

> People might say to us: But why have you tolerated it for so long? To that, I would reply that the attention of the music publishers was awakened to this kind of counterfeiting by the prodigious growth it has undergone in these recent years. Paris, gentlemen, has no fewer than ten special makers of mechanical pianos; it also has ten makers of musical boxes, tableaux, and clocks. In Mirecourt, a village in the *département* of the Vosges, they annually make 2 million barrel organs.[9]

Faced with this proliferation of mechanical instruments, the affair took on the dimension of a collective struggle. The Escudier brothers obtained the support of other publishers, as well as that of renowned composers (Auber, Berlioz, Gounod, Halévy, Rossini . . .). These composers signed the following manifesto:

> It would be a grave error to believe that the more popular a piece of music is, the more it enriches the publisher and adds to the composer's renown. When a piece of music is too well known, people tire of it, they stop performing it, they no longer buy it. . . . This weariness that replaces enthusiasm is especially fatal when success, instead of being maintained in the realm of taste and among the upper classes, descends and is made vulgar. . . . The mechanical-piano will very quickly lead new music to this latter and deplorable limit of success; through it, music will age before its time, and, if we allow it to reproduce new compositions, it will become a cause of decadence for art and ruin for those whose existence depends on art.

It is remarkable that we find here, perhaps for the first time in the history of Western music, the idea that success is a *threat* to the creation of "art." This is not only—as a current prejudice would have it—because a composition that becomes popular too quickly is suspect in its quality. It is rather the idea, so unusual, and also so *new*, that a new work might risk something in being *consumed* too quickly and before its time, in being denied a kind of time for maturation or period of latency . . .

Obviously, the signers of the manifesto fear being *dispossessed* by a sort of immediate availability of their works. Dispossessed of what, precisely? The draft of a reply (which we will have to elaborate later on) is given, from a strictly legal standpoint, by the decision of the criminal court of the Seine; the judges, faced with an unusual situation on which previous laws and legal precedents remained silent, had recourse to reasoning by analogy: they decided that Debain's boards constituted a "publication."[10] And the verdict was based on Article 425 of the Penal Code of 1810, stipulating that "any publication . . . which disregards the laws and regulations relative to the property of authors, is a counterfeit."

Indeed, probably because of the judges' uncertainty, the court punished Debain only with a fine that was largely symbolic. But the analogy was set in place, and it would make its way: mechanical reproduction was a form of *writing* that competed with traditional publication by making musical notation outdated. Sidelined. We can understand better, from this point of view, why the signers of the manifesto against mechanical music could think that their art was threatened with *vulgarization*: if notation became potentially obsolete, the whole hierarchy of the musical sciences—composers, interpreters, listeners—risked collapsing along with it.

Engramelle spoke of *notage* when referring to his cylinders. And these phonographs before-the-letter were indeed forms of notation or writing; they did have a scriptural quality. But their signs, their letters, no longer summoned any decoding, any reading. Should we see phonography in its general sense, then, as an *illegible writing*, as the courts would soon do? A kind of Braille whose touch would be reserved for mechanical organs? These questions will keep us company for a long time.

Whatever the case may be, in the Escudier vs. Debain affair, the two parties appealed twice. But before the Court of Appeal could hand down a definitive judgment, the instrument maker and the publishers had reached an amicable agreement: Debain, in return for the sum of 60,000 francs, acquired the exclusive right to reproduce mechanically the works that the publishers owned.[11] From then on, Debain could legally subpoena his own competitors, makers of mechanical instruments; between 1861 and 1863, he obtained a series of injunctions that confirmed his monopoly.

Music in Braille

This legal protection granted to Debain was short-lived. To accommodate the economic interests of Switzerland, a country that was a major producer of mechanical instruments and with which it was getting ready to conclude a treaty, France undertook to host an international convention in 1864 freeing from all restriction "reproductions of musical compositions by the mechanism of music boxes or other similar instruments." The law in question was voted in with a strong majority and came into effect on May 16, 1866; its single article stipulated: "The fabrication and sale of instruments serving to reproduce mechanically musical airs, which are in the private domain, *do not constitute* the act of musical counterfeiting, in the sense specified and punished by the law of July 19, 1793."

This law, which revised recent legal precedents by deregulating the mechanical reproduction of music, was clearly the result of diplomatic pressure; thus, when the draft of the law was debated in the Senate, Mérimée declared: "We have to envision the possibility of breaking the treaty with Switzerland if the law is rejected." Once adopted, this law would continue to regulate the mechanical reproduction of music until 1917.[12]

Between the adoption and the rescinding of such a principle of *free sonorous reproduction*, between 1866 and 1917, then, some of the most fascinating legal debates about our instruments for listening took place. These decades witnessed the birth or development of various techniques for the mechanization of music, the most important of which was the pneumatic system that activated the keys of a keyboard by means of perforated rolls. Aside from the famous *pianolas*, with their levers controlling tempo and other nuances, there were apparatuses like the *melograph-melotrope* pair, which reproduced with a high degree of fidelity the dynamics and agogics of the greatest pianists. Constructed by Jules Carpentier for the International Exhibition of Electricity that took place in Paris in 1880, the melograph, perfected in 1887, was a kind of "telegraphic recorder" linked to an ensemble of electrical sensors placed beneath the keys of a keyboard: it noted down the playing by means of lines on a continuous strip of paper, which became the master for a perforated card that could be played by the melotrope.

The companies that commercialized these apparatuses offered their clients subscriptions that bore a strong resemblance to our present-day record libraries. A prospectus of the Aeolian firm, specializing in pianolas, offered the following option: "In return for the payment of a sum of 40 francs for a period of three months, the client will have the right to take out all the rolls he likes, in a series of 12 rolls at a time, which he can exchange as often as he likes and keep for a maximum of one month."

Faced with this situation, the Employer's Syndicate of Music Publishers decided to institute legal proceedings in 1893 against certain makers of perforated cards. This trial, which was known as the "Trial of Mechanical Instruments," completed the defeat of the publishers and confirmed for a time the validity of the 1866 law. The ruling handed down by the Court of Paris on January 9, 1895, provided a negative response to the question of whether perforated cards constituted a *publication*; the Court decided

> that the notation of perforated cards is as varied as the instruments to which these cards are applied, and even as varied as the dimensions of these instruments; that supposing an individual can learn one of these notations, he cannot learn the others, and that even by admitting for a few initiates a general intuition of the procedure, the truth will always be that musical works will never be publishable in this form for the musical public addressed by the plaintiffs [i.e., the publishers].

In other words, rolls, cards, boards, and cylinders were not, in the eyes of the court, a notation of music, inasmuch as they could be "read" only by one type of machine; they made up a kind of *machine-language*, a writing that was too idiomatic—that is to say, speaking etymologically, too *idiotic*—to be decoded and interpreted. This was not only because it remained incomprehensible to musicians and music-lovers, as Mérimée had suggested in his report to the Senate one year before the adoption of the 1866 law. For, if it were only a question of a different "alphabet," we might rightly wonder, as Mérimée did: "If a publisher decided to publish, without authorization, the French book of a living author in Greek characters, would we hesitate to condemn him as a counterfeiter?" No: in the opinion of the judges in 1895, far from being a strange or foreign language, *notage* destined for mechanical instruments was not writing at all. For the very reason that it was indissociable from the machine to which it had been destined, it remained caught in its moving parts, incapable of "expressing" anything in a different context; in other words, according to the terms of the ruling of the Court of Paris: "Perforated cards, in order to be mobile parts, are no less integral parts of the organism [*sic*, meaning the machine], and constitute . . . the soul of the instrument."

Something of this reasoning could still be found in the lines that, many years later (in 1934), Adorno devoted to "The Form of the Phonograph Record": the record, he wrote, "is covered with curves, a delicately scribbled, utterly illegible writing, which here and there forms more plastic figures for reasons that remain obscure to the layman upon listening."[13] In other words (and I will come back to this), the visible grooves on the record *no longer convey the reason* (as musical notation does) for what we hear.

Whatever the case may be, despite the strength of the evidence, despite the lasting resonance it had, the judges' argumentation is eminently debatable: it is not because a notation remains reserved for an extremely restricted use that it loses its nature as script. And the lawyer Georges Sbriglia, commenting on the decision of the Court of Paris in a work that was published some ten years later, was right to contest it by using recourse to the analogy with "the admirable Braille method, thanks to which the blind can write or print prose, numbers, or music." Sbriglia asserted: "That is a procedure that is indeed not accessible to everyone, that is not addressed to sight but to another sense, touch. Who would claim, however, that there is not a real publication there?"

Sbriglia could indeed have placed his finger, if I may say so, on the profound reason forbidding us to regard *notage* as a writing: what mechanical instruments called into question was the primacy of the visible in the comprehension of music, in its interpretation. What they profoundly subverted was a certain *ideality* of the musical letter.[14] Their writing was addressed to a blind, tactile, groping body: that of the *ordinary person* who, turning a crank or manipulating levers and buttons, still felt in his limbs an unprecedented elasticity of musical time.

The Phonograph in Court

It is generally agreed that the phonograph was invented by Thomas Alva Edison in 1877. This invention was closely linked to the developments of telephony and telegraphy; one of the motivations of Edison and his collaborators was to succeed at recording telephonic messages. Thus the phonograph was first associated with the *spoken voice*. In one of the first notes recorded by Edison about his invention, we read that "the spkg vibrations are indented nicely & theres no doubt that I shall be able to store & reproduce automatically at any future time the human voice perfectly."[15]

So the phonograph was, in the mind of its inventor, an instrument that was essentially *speaking*. In fact, once the invention was perfected and industrialized, advertisements for the phonograph used the image of an opera singer by preference: thus in the beginning of the twentieth century the "Victor Talking Machine Company" stated, on an announcement showing a record next to the famous singer Caruso, that "the Victor record of Caruso's voice *is* Caruso as truly as Caruso himself"; this message was conveyed in another way by the famous dog listening to "his master's voice." Phonographic fidelity was measured above all by its capacity to reproduce the voice or, even better, *speech*. And that is why, in the first trials involving the phonograph, the dividing line between speech and music was the deciding factor.

It is precisely this distinction, between "pure" music and words (possibly accompanied by music), which made it possible to go beyond the French law of 1866, which regarded as licit the mechanical reproduction of "musical airs" without authorization from the authors. In fact, the phonograph, with its capacity to reproduce the voice (spoken or sung), opened a breach in the legislation concerning mechanical instruments. The voice had remained outside the reach of previous inventions; cylinders, rolls, and other perforated cards could not capture it. Whereas Edison's machine, by recording speech as well as simple sounds and noises, inaugurated the era of the reproducibility of *all* possible sonorities, human and nonhuman. And that is why it changed drastically the liberal legal concepts that, until around 1900, left the field wide open for makers of mechanical instruments. But, as you'll see, by doing so it contributed to extending the circle of a *legalism of the sonorous* that today encompasses the most commonplace sounds forming the landscape that surrounds us.

In 1905 an obscure individual by the name of Vives organized in France the defense of representatives of *living* music (today we'd say "live"), that is to say, composers and publishers.[16] Vives, a retired civil servant, obtained a power of attorney from publishers authorizing him to institute proceedings in their name, but solely at his own risk, against makers of phonographs. In exchange, publishers undertook to entrust him with managing their rights for phonographic reproduction if these rights came to be recognized. Armed with this power of attorney, Vives brought action against the Pathé company and chose as his lawyer Raymond Poincaré, who pleaded that the record was indeed a publication, since it mechanically reproduced *speech*. The lawyer for Pathé, however, claimed that the record remained in the framework of the 1866 law on mechanical instruments. In 1903, Vives lost his court case on its first hearing. But he appealed and won the case in 1905. This judgment ensured Vives a prosperous retirement, since he was soon made head of a "Collection Bureau" for rights to mechanical reproduction, a kind of *office of live music*.

According to certain much-debated sources, it seems that Vives managed to conquer the reticence of the judges quite simply by *letting the phonograph take the stand*:

> They say . . . that Vives had a record made for them and that he played it for them in the course of the hearing, by means of a phonograph he had brought with him. This is the gist of the text he is said to have recorded: "Mr. President, Your Honors, do I have to insult you so you'll finally understand that I am a publication?" This was a revelation for the Court, which understood that this apparatus could not be compared to the music box, which does not speak!

Whatever its authenticity, this anecdote is likely to be true solely because of the fascinating *prosopopoeia* it stages. For it is indeed the phonograph, a *speaking* instrument par excellence, that *takes the stand* here and testifies for itself. At the bar, the phonograph speaks and says, "I say that I speak." Can you imagine the deathly silence that must have welcomed this ghostly voice? Still, the fact is that, beginning with this affair, phonography, *insofar as it spoke*, became a publication.[17]

The rights of *dramatic* authors were protected, then; reproduction of their works became equivalent to counterfeiting. And if the makers of phonographs still had an open field for recordings of music alone, that was meager compensation, since their catalogues were made up in large part of songs and operatic airs.

So the phonograph contributed to extending the field of artistic protection to the realm of mechanical reproductions. But its time at court also had another consequence, one more difficult to grasp: henceforth, our phonographic listenings would be inscribed in a regulated legal framework whose signs, discreet but quite visible, would be the "labels" stuck on records, bearing the trademarks of the copyright holders. Labels that Vives and his office sold to companies like Pathé for several million francs, and that proved that payment for rights of reproduction had been made.

Rights for Reproduction and Radio Broadcast

Vives' bureau first of all gave birth to an International Office of Mechanical Publication [the Bureau international de l'édition mécanique, or BIEM] in 1927, then to the Society of Rights to Mechanical Reproduction (SDRM) founded in July 1935.[18] But the technological developments underway, ever since the end of the nineteenth century, did not concern only the aforementioned rights of reproduction, results of the widening of the *right to publication* instituted by the Revolutionary decree of 1793. It also affected the *right of representation* established in 1791. And, here again, some time was needed for the *public* performance of musical works by means of mechanical instruments to be recognized through a series of cases as being actual performances, in the sense of the Revolutionary decree.

Thus, in 1881, a certain Huguet had been prosecuted for having made a mechanical organ function in his wooden-horse merry-go-round in Auteuil, hence reproducing musical airs in public.[19] Although the Paris Court, in its ruling of April 22, 1881, had dismissed all charges against Huguet (with the reason that his carrousel did not constitute "a performance or a theatrical representation"), the Supreme Court reversed the ruling by deciding that he had indeed committed a misdemeanor of illicit representation by "publicly performing, without formal permission from the authors, their literary and musical works, which have not entered the public domain."

At first, so-called serious (or "classical") music was less likely than other kinds of music to be *publicly* represented by these machines. Although the phonograph let operatic voices or virtuoso pianists be heard in the privacy of one's own home, it did not constitute (yet) an instrument of *recital*. A borderline case can be cited, though, as it was recounted by Sbriglia, of a concert given by Strauss in Madison Square Garden in 1890: "During the performance of a polka entitled 'The Phonograph' and dedicated to Edison, the Viennese maestro, to the applause of the public which demanded an encore, raised his baton . . . but the orchestra did not move, and the polka was repeated by twelve machines that the Phonographic Society had placed around the platform of the orchestra."

With the developments of "theatrophones" and other apparatus transmitting music long distance, the situation changed: allied with telephony, phonography drastically changed the delicate frontier between private and public performance. That is why, the same night that Strauss was conducting his concert at Madison Square Garden, "a host, giving a soiree in Morristown, used as dance music the orchestra that was playing twenty or thirty miles away." Little by little, the phenomenon of long-distance transmission began to affect "serious" music. So it was taken seriously by the courts. In 1899, Giuseppe Verdi won a trial against the Belgian Society of Private Telephony that, during the Exhibition of Electricity in Brussels, had placed, in the concert hall of the Society of Artistic Concerts, receivers allowing people to listen via telephone to a program on which a tune from *Rigoletto* was featured.[20] The judgment clearly established that a long-distance transmission was a performance of the work.

Mechanical instruments involved the right to reproduction, then, as well as the right to representation. And it is this reassertion of the authority of the author—of his *authorship*—in the sphere of (tele)phonography that various international conventions register, down to the middle of the twentieth century.[21]

We, who listen a century later, are of course the inheritors of this brief and recent history of our instruments for listening. For, after having experienced a setback, before revolutionary advances (with the law of 1866 establishing a free sonorous reproduction), these auditory prostheses that are boards or phonographs were also reinterpreted in light of an authenticity and authorship, a precision and effectiveness, of which Romanticism would never have dared to dream. Or rather for a long time they kept (and probably will continue today to keep) the remnant trace of an original ambivalence: between, on one hand, a *blind capture* of music that does not respond to or account for anything; and, on the other, the ghostly echo of the name and speech of the author, of "his master's voice." The problems Stravinsky and Schoenberg had with the music industry are the best testimony to this *divided* nature of our prostheses.

Stravinsky, Schoenberg, and Pirates

In March 1949, Stravinsky lost a trial that had begun in October 1947. It pitted him against the Leeds Music Corporation, and concerned "arrangement." This affair, the ramifications of which go back to around 1910, condenses most of the musical issues raised in this first half of the twentieth century by what Adorno would call the *culture industry*. It also testifies to Stravinsky's ambivalent attitude toward the technological system constituted by instruments for the mechanical reproduction of music. For Stravinsky, in effect, these instruments were *both* a means of asserting his authorial ownership *and* a dispossessing and disappropriating machine.

From the *Firebird* ballet music, commissioned by Diaghilev, Stravinsky drew a first concert suite, which was published in Russia in 1911 by a certain Jurgenson.[22] With the legal difficulties raised by the Russian Revolution (the Soviet government no longer subscribing to international conventions regulating artistic property), Stravinsky lost legal ownership of his work, which was no longer protected. Thus he wrote, in 1918–19, a *new version* (an auto-arrangement, if you like) in order to get it back. Without managing to do so.[23]

In 1945, Stravinsky, having become an American citizen, decided to write a third "new suite" of *Firebird* (the copyright to which would this time be assured him) and to sell it to the Leeds Music Corporation. But Stravinsky was once again the victim of a form of dispossession: he attacked Leeds for having had an arrangement made, without his authorization, entitled *Summer*

Moon, after the theme of the "dance of the princesses" in *Firebird*.

Summer Moon is a slow foxtrot, with lyrics by John Klenner: *Summer Moon, you bring the end of my love story. . . .*[24] The publishers first displayed beneath the title the untruthful statement, "adapted from the *Firebird* Suite by Igor Stravinsky." As for the arranger, a certain Spielman, he is said to have declared before the court that "by using other harmonies . . . he still expressed the 'same sentiments.'" *Summer Moon* was explicitly destined for the jukebox market, as Stravinsky recalled in a declaration that he had broadcast: "These vulgar Broadway people . . . had the idea of taking melodies from *Firebird* . . . and wrapping the garbage up in the title 'Summer Moon'. . . . The intention was to attract the 'jukebox market.'"

Stravinsky's indignation seems legitimate, as he was faced with this rampant misappropriation. However, Stravinsky did not hesitate to carry out auto-arrangements intended to ensure him a reappropriation of his own work. He had made, as they would say today in a different vocabulary, his own *remix*. And he did this, by means of this *same* practice of arrangement that he afterwards associated with a certain "market" for mechanical music, for the sake of affirming his authorial ownership.

That the mechanization of music (or more generally, the culture industry) can *also* be an instrument of consolidation of authorial values is illustrated by the well-known episode that links Stravinsky with the Pleyel firm. Stravinsky himself relates, in his *Autobiography*, the period (1921–22) when his "connection" began with the Pleyel company, which had suggested he "make a transcription" of his works for a mechanical piano called the "Pleyela." And here we hear him singing the praises of machines that allow us to *limit the freedom of the interpreter*:

> In order to prevent the distortion of my compositions by future interpreters, I had always been anxious to find a means of imposing some restriction on the notorious liberty, especially

widespread today, which prevents the public from obtaining a correct idea of the author's intentions. This possibility was now afforded by the rolls of the mechanical piano, and, a little later, by gramophone records. (*Igor Stravinsky: An Autobiography* [New York: Simon and Schuster, 1936], 101.)

Stravinsky inherits concepts issuing from the development of copyright in the second half of the nineteenth century, but shifts them and reinscribes them in the sphere of mechanical precision. He may even express the ultimate and ambivalent truth about them: a certain complicity between the notion of authorial interpretation and mechanized fixity; a certain collusion, then, between the affirmation of the author's authority and the industry of musical reproduction. All the arguments (full of pathos) about the loss of the "living" and "live" interpretation are only a strict inversion of this *structural* complicity, the *principle* of which they do not in the least change. Ricordi's speeches were the proof of this; the labels sold by Vives were the tangible signs of this, the *seals*.

It was a representative of the Society of Rights to Mechanical Reproduction (SDRM) who, on July 18, 1936, sent Stravinsky a document describing the illicit exploitation and deformations of *The Firebird* in a film bearing the same name, produced by Warner Brothers: "The music of the final dance is repeated in the beginning of the film. Then, fragments of the original score are introduced and interrupted haphazardly, according to the whims of the plot." Fragmentation, inversion of the original flow: that seems to be the law of exposing music to the mechanical medium of film or to the culture industry in general. Which, while giving authors the means to contain it or restrain it, feeds on the very strength of the principle of *arrangement*. And the disappropriating power of mechanization would give a strangely familiar (if uncanny, *unheimlich*) musical image to Stravinsky, who had made this principle the very motivation for his writing. In Schoenberg's words (with whose critical attitude about this we are familiar), Stravinsky "constantly finds something to 'collect' in Bach, in Scarlatti, in Clementi, or in another musician";[25] Stravinsky was in a way a *sampler* before the letter, and the list of his samplings, borrowings, or citations would resemble the credits in liner notes on rap CDs.

It was probably the "prehistoric" part of Walt Disney's famous *Fantasia* that presented Stravinsky with this unsettling mirror of the disappropriating power of arrangement in the most troubling way. This time, it was *Le Sacre du Printemps* that was involved. And, once again, the question of rights was in the foreground. For, as Stravinsky recalls in *Expositions and Developments*,[26] when, in 1938, the offices of Walt Disney sought authorization to use the score, "the request was accompanied by a gentle warning that if permission were withheld the music would be used anyway." Like *Firebird*, *Le Sacre du Printemps* had been published in Russia, and so was not protected by copyright in the United States. And here again, the music underwent *arrangements* that, to paraphrase Berlioz, were so many *derangements*; Stravinsky says:

> I saw the film . . . in a Hollywood studio at Christmas time in 1939. . . . I remember someone offering me a score and, when I said I had my own, the someone saying, "But it is all changed." It was indeed. The instrumentation had been improved by such stunts as having the horns play their glissandi an octave higher in the *Danse de la terre*. The order of the pieces had been shuffled, too, and the most difficult of them eliminated. (166)

What upsets Stravinsky here is precisely what bothered Schoenberg in Stravinsky's "plunderings."

Schoenberg, however, wrote (and said) very little about Stravinsky (the same cannot be said the other way round). The rare occurrences of his name are thus revealing, especially in the few scattered pages that Schoenberg devoted to the question of copyright.

The English edition of *Style and Idea* includes several texts explicitly devoted to copyright, including a manuscript written in English at the end of the 1940s. Following this manuscript text, the German edition also adds two other pieces to the file:[27] a brief "elucidation," dated February 18, 1949, where we can read that Schoenberg thinks it his "duty" to reveal his "opinion of Mr. Stravinsky's suit against the Leeds Company," as well as a draft of a letter to Stravinsky's lawyer, in which Schoenberg declares:

> True artists live according to strict rules of a code of honor. . . . It is precisely for this code of honor that Stravinsky is waging a fight against these parasites for whom art is nothing but a way of earning money. I remember the first time I heard the news about Mr. Str.'s foray into the market of musical automatons, and already at the time I had the suspicion that, through blackmail, he had been forced to tolerate the violence done to his works. Wasn't it posed in these terms: "You are not protected; we can do it without your authorization" . . . ? Of course: he was not protected, since the copyright law does not serve to protect the author. . . . It should be called, "copyright of pirates."

Once we have gotten over our surprise at seeing Schoenberg step forward as a *defender* of Stravinsky, we must, in order to take stock of what is at stake in his stance, regard these documents in light of the other texts in *Style and Idea* devoted to copyright. Among the musical propositions that Schoenberg, in 1919, had sent to Adolf Loos so that they would figure in his "Guide-Lines for a Ministry of Art,"[28] the third one has to do with the rights to intellectual property. Schoenberg calls for these to be placed "in every respect on a par with rights in all other property," that is to say that we recognize, in this domain too, "permanently inheritable rights."

If we compare this demand to a manuscript from the end of the 1940s entitled "Copyright," we can understand how it is a characteristic feature by which Schoenberg characterizes musical works: the music publisher, he says, "is seldom forced to make improvements," since "the works are finished [abgeschlossen: closed] and ready to be sold" (Style and Idea, 498). By thus excluding arrangements and adaptations from the regime of "serious" musical productions, Schoenberg, unlike Schumann, asserts that the work, already perfect, cannot be perfected any further.

In 1912, however, in "Parsifal and Copyright," Schoenberg's discourse included a few additional twists that deserve our attention. It was a matter of knowing "whether a prolongation of the copyright protection period for Parsifal should be attempted," according to which performances of the opera were forbidden anywhere but in Bayreuth. At first, Schoenberg declares that Siegfried, Wagner's son, does not have the right to "ignore the last wish of his father" (and he adds, "least of all the son of such a father"). Exclusive rights should thus be renewed in order to "fulfill Wagner's will, which has to be held as sacred [heilig] there"; they should "see that it prevails without second thoughts," Schoenberg continues, "even in matters where such second thoughts may be a downright artistic necessity" (Style and Idea, 491–92).

What is the necessity for this reserve? By keeping rigidly to principles [prinzipienstarr], Siegfried ran the risk of being faithful to his father's last will and testament "at the expense of art" [auf Kosten der Kunst]. And thus of being unfaithful, through his too great fidelity, of lacking what that father, "the great revolutionary," saw as "the last word in piety toward the masters": namely, "ridding [befreien] their works' true essence of whatever in it is merely mortal [sterblich], in order to let their immortality register in all the greater purity." Wagner Sr., as Schoenberg in fact recalls, "found altering the composer's express wishes not only within the bounds of piety but in fact a commandment. He was

certainly the first to propose changing Beethoven's scoring"
(*Style and Idea*, 492).

The analysis of these reinstrumentations of Beethoven's symphonies (especially the Ninth) has yet to be undertaken: it will
be for us a matter of listening; we will literally hear in it our ears
being fabricated. But the fact remains that, in a gesture that is
now unquestionably Schumann-like, Schoenberg—who would
finally decide *against* prolonging Bayreuth's monopoly over *Parsifal*—seems to be saying that the *essence* (the timeless idea) of a
work is *at the end, at the horizon* of its more or less arranging or
disarranging variations. And he justifies his decision by remarks
on style:

> A style cannot arise when the object around which it is sup-
> posed to develop is kept away from living influences. For style
> is not . . . something that we preserve in all purity [*ein Treube-
> wahrtes*]. How is it to exist, if the work of art behaves as people
> behaved in 1890, whereas the listener's sensations are the sen-
> sations of people in 1912? (*Style and Idea*, 494 [translation
> slightly modified])

Behind this claim of an eternal artistic property (eternally
transmissible without damage or derangements) Schoenberg has
opened here, as if despite himself, the space of a question that is
uniquely our own: How should we hear Wagner (or Schoenberg
for that matter) today? In other words, what are the conditions
for a *style of listening*? And what can we do, with all our disks and
listeners' instruments, with what we must call the Schoenbergian
"double bind": arrange me, keep me alive, but without touching
my heritage?

The Furtwängler Ruling and Subsidiary Laws

Let's let that question resonate for a little while. For, after
Schoenberg and Stravinsky, the sphere of what authorship com-
prised was extended by lawyers in a startling way. In France, the

Furtwängler ruling of January 4, 1964, marked recognition of a true quality of *oeuvre* in the recorded interpretation of a "performing artist."[29] And, after the status of the interpreter was clarified, the record producer soon had his creation protected in similar terms.[30] The courts tend to broaden the status of the work. But faced with these relationships of proximity that increasingly make a semi-authorial status influence all our intermediaries and representatives, I sense the inevitable question dawning in you: *What about us?* Will we listeners end up, as the last in line or at the end of the race, having an *authority* that is explicitly formulated and codified, that is to say, recognized and regulated?

Patience, we're coming to that. Soon we will meet a distant descendant of the Zachariases and Tyszkiewiczes, who will find himself before the court with our present instruments for listening. But, before we greet him, we will have to follow into its recent developments the *integrative* tendency of author's rights. A tendency that leads the courts to have to rule on—and hence to include in the legal sphere—*everything that is audible* here on this earth, including the most ordinary and the "freest" sounds surrounding us.

Trademarking a Sound (Harley-Davidson in the Sonic Landscape)

After interpretations and recordings, it would be *sounds*, simply sounds *as such*, that would be granted legal protection.

Protecting a sound does not, however, speak for itself. In fact, the legal apparatus of copyright is traditionally *melocentric*: melody is alone in being entirely the object of an "appropriation," that is to say, it is assigned to an author who is the owner of it, while other musical parameters—harmony and rhythm—are taken into account only as they interact with melody.[31] As for sound, as for timbre, they simply do not enter the equation.

How can a sound, *distinct from any reference to a work or to part of a work*, become a musical creation that can be protected, then? Since the quality of authoriality in this domain seems eminently problematic in the eyes of the law, the extension of artistic ownership would occur on other grounds.

This evolution is recent: it's not until the 1980s, with the spread of the practice of sampling—which allows one to take more or less short excerpts from a recording without any loss of quality—that sound was truly *detached* from the compositional architecture or layout that included it. Some commercial companies offer ready-made *samples catalogues* for rap or techno musicians. These *sounds*, which are the object of a kind of musical commerce of *raw material*, bring up the problem of their ownership, that is to say of the protection of the rights of their *first creators*, before the sounds were integrated into a composition signed by an author.[32]

One solution that is sometimes envisaged consists in making sound a *registered trademark*. The American company Harley-Davidson tried to do so for the sound of its engines when it submitted its case to the United States Patent and Trademark Office in February 1994. Harley-Davidson was not the first company to seek the status of registered trademark for a sound. The main precedent is undoubtedly that of the National Broadcasting Company (NBC) in 1950, with its sonorous "logo" comprising three notes (*sol, mi, do*) played by chimes (these three notes, G-E-C in Anglo-Saxon musical notation, were in fact a kind of sonorous acronym for the General Electric Corporation, which owned NBC at the time). More strictly *sonorous* (without any reference to musical notation), there is also the lion's roar of Metro-Goldwyn-Mayer, another example of a registered trademark. But these precedents, although they do exist, are still quite rare.

Whatever the case may be, as the lawyer for one of Harley's competitors (the Japanese firm Honda) stressed, "It's very difficult to imagine a world where the sound of a running engine is an exclusive property right."[33] Moreover, the difficulty of the Harley case is that, unlike the NBC chimes or the lion's roar of

Metro-Goldwyn-Mayer, the noise of a motorcycle's exhaust is not a *fixed* sonority (if the company wanted to protect a *recording* of this noise, it could easily rely on the laws regulating the property rights of recordings); it is a matter rather of ownership of a *type of sound, beyond its infinite possible contextual variations* (depending on the model, on how the motorcycle rider uses it, on the speed, etc.).

The very existence of this debate bears witness to the increasing ascendancy of law and legislation over what could be called our "sonorous landscape." The Harley affair is, in a way, the auditory counterpart to the debates that recently agitated the laws concerning photography.[34] After that we can wonder, along with Henri Cartier-Bresson: "Do we still have the right to look or not? What photos do we want to preserve of our history, of our society, of our daily life?"[35] Or rather: Do we have the right to *let people see*? Publicly to exchange our gazes? And our listenings?

You are imagining a world where we could no longer "look at reality," as Cartier-Bresson says, with precisely these optical instruments that reveal it to us. Well, the other part of that world, its audible side, would be a universe peopled with sounds that are all "trademarked." I can already see the ghost of the poor Pierre Schaeffer, who, when he was alive, haunted train stations in order to record his *Étude aux chemins de fer*, with the avowed aim of making locomotives "sing" in a concrete musical work: Schaeffer, today, might indeed find himself *out of work* [désoeuvré, literally "un-worked," meaning having nothing to do].

You smile at my grave prophet's face. But perhaps you have not measured as I have the consequences of this evolution for our listenings. Just as our gazes have a number of instruments (cameras, video cameras, and other prostheses), our ears are likewise *outfitted* as never before. And, from Pierre Schaeffer down to the DJs of today, this equipment opens the possibility, for every listener, of making his own listenings *recognized*: of reproducing them, spreading them, that is to say *publishing* them, in order to hear them, exchange them, comment on them—in short, to construct a *critical* culture of listening. But at the same time the extension of the law that accompanies or pursues these technical developments tends to lower all our listenings to the status of *quotations.*

On the Right to Quotation in Music (John Oswald, the Listener)

A unique listener by the name of John Oswald has tried to promote his listenings to the status of *quasi-oeuvres.* This Canadian composer, who recently enjoyed some celebrity through his "sonorous pillagings" or *plunderphonics* (to use the term he himself created), is a kind of distant descendant of Zacharias, but one endowed with a modern and effective instrumentarium of listening.

"I began as a listener," John Oswald says.[36] A wonderful fact that all of us would like to admit, to adopt . . . But if he can say this so calmly, it is because this particular listener did not begin by listening and then go on to do something else (becoming a composer, an interpreter, a critic . . .). It is *as a listener* that he continues to practice music. And to *sign* his work.

Oswald is a listening artist, then. Not a skilled, "scholarly" kind of listening, deciphering works to discover what they are meant to convey. No, his art of listening has formed and developed starting from his very insufficiencies ("like most kids, I had a short attention span," he confides). And, with this background of a *lack of attention*, Oswald has developed *techniques* of listening that he calls "active":

> I played classical music 33s at the speed of 78s, and . . . the structure clearly appeared to me in a kind of auditory version of panoramic vision. . . . And often I'd realize that I preferred listening to musical pieces at speeds other than the one they were made for.

The plunge is taken when Oswald decides to preserve what he calls his "manipulative listenings," which are increasingly complex. In 1989, he collected some of his active listener's manipulations on a CD entitled *Plunderphonics*. The disc was distributed for free. On the sleeve (also composed by the "author"), the head of Michael Jackson is grafted (with his leather jacket) onto a young girl's naked body. The result is a court trial: all the recordings would have to be destroyed, along with the master.[37]

Oswald, however, speaks of "respect" in the practice of what he calls "electroquoting." But he readily admits that "quotation marks aren't used in the audio medium." And that is in fact where the shoe pinches. Zacharias had sensed it when, long ago, he had suggested importing footnotes into the musical field. Only he had neglected this fundamental difference between music and literature: namely, that while footnotes, like quotation marks, are text, there are no quotation marks *in music*, any more than there are *musical* signatures. Even if Bach and so many others were able to encrypt their authorial name into musical notation (according to the Anglo-Saxon principle that attributes a letter to each note),[38] *we do not hear* their signature as such. And, from then on, listening to a musical quotation, listening with our ears alone, without seeing anything or reading anything, is always to listen to a *stolen object*. The "right to quotation," in music, suffers from such a fact. For if this right, even in the other arts, is surely the most poorly defined of all, it is in music that it is most problematic.

The uncertainty of the law is evident everywhere. Thus Henri Desbois writes, quite seriously, in *Le droit d'auteur en France*: "In order to satisfy the obligation of mentioning the author and the source, the composer should place an opening bracket on the staff, and the interpreter should keep his bow immobile or raise his hands from the keyboard in order to read out the reference."[39] *Sic.* And the eminent lawyer adds, concerning the purpose of quotation: "Composers neither argue nor discuss." According to legal doctrine, musicians are incapable of reference or thought . . .

Beyond these naïve statements (which are nonetheless far from being free from a whole ideology of music), the question that should keep us occupied is: Is there truly, when it comes to quotation, a *structural* difference between music and the plastic arts or cinema, for example? In other words: could an image, *in itself*, show that it is a quotation, without any recourse to a text, a title, a signature, a caption? You will tell me that letters are also images, that they do not make us leave the field of vision. True. But then it would be enough, for example, as lawyers who aren't music lovers suggest, to read out loud the footnotes of a Zacharias to make a case for "faithful use" of his musical collages, for scholarly or educational purposes. We would still have not abandoned the sensorial domain of hearing. In fact, I don't think there is any more *intrinsic* distance between music and words than there is between images and letters. The reason for the legal difficulties of musical quotation is to be sought elsewhere: in the heritage of Romanticism, probably, which invented the notion of *pure* music (or *absolute* music, that is, without words or texts) and which made it the *paradigm* for musical art.

Once the hypothesis of a singularity *by nature* affecting musical quotation is discarded, we can begin to wonder about the consequences of the legal *singularization* that restricts its right more than in other domains. What seems more worrying for us listeners is exclusion from the critical space of the musical field pure and simple. From a legal point of view, everything happens as if there were no more room for a musical criticism *in music*: any work that includes musical quotations is either a *new* musical work, or an *adaptation*; thus music criticism, relegated to the "extramusical," becomes the exclusive business of words, and language.

CHAPTER 4 *Listening (to Listening):*
The Making of the Modern Ear

What might the *responsibility of a listener* be today, in the era of digital recording and sampling, who, far from receiving a musical work as "something to be heard," would assume *responsibility for its making*? In what sense could one say, taking into account an increasing *instrumentation* of listening (by radio, tape, recordable CD, sampler, etc.), that *it is listeners who make music* (just as Marcel Duchamp said, "It is the viewers who make paintings")? How can one accede to the notion of listening *as arrangement,* and of the work as it is (and *must* be) as something that is *still to come*?

We must reweave the scattered reasons that have accompanied us to this point—the place for arrangement, the legal status of musical works—in order to let them say what they have to say about *the listening that musical modernity configures*. Where, in fact, does a certain "structural listening" come from, a *great listening* corresponding to *great music,* with whose form and details it is supposed to agree perfectly?

This will be, finally, *our* history, the story of the listeners we are today. But if this history that I am getting ready to relate to you summons data that can be called "sociological," I would also, and perhaps especially, like to deduce it from *the works that there are,* and from what, in them, *awaits us and includes us.* Two connecting threads weave through this history to begin with:

one, now familiar, of arrangement, of those arrangers who sign their listenings; and one, somewhat stranger, of a theater or a stage where we meet *characters listening*, where we, listeners and spectators, go *see them and hear them listening*.

Before reaching this fable that tells about *us*, allow me to begin with the end: with the *moral*.

Types of Listening (Adorno's Diagnosis)

We are indebted to Adorno's *Introduction to the Sociology of Music*[1] for a typology of *attitudes of listening*—a typology that for its author is almost equivalent to a definition of the sociology of music as such: "Asked to say offhand what a sociology of music is, one would probably start by defining it as knowledge of the relation between music and the socially organized individuals who listen to it" (1). After that, the whole question is what is meant by "music itself." For Adorno, it seems that it is above all individual *works*. That is the presupposition that governs his inventory, his cartography of the "typical modes of conduct in listening to music under the conditions that prevail in present-day society" (1). His typology depends, then, on a *history*, the history of the progressive emergence of the notion of a *work*.

"Accordingly," Adorno writes, "the canon," the norm, "guiding the construction of the types [in this typology] does not—as in the case of purely subjectively directed empirical findings—refer exclusively to tastes, preferences, aversions, and habits of the audience" (3). So it will not be a question here of a simple "compilation of inarticulate facts," a simple statistical gathering of the opinions given by a panel of listeners. And we can readily agree with Adorno that no collection of "information"—as objective and stripped of prejudice as it may be—contains in itself, intrinsically, the criteria that allow us to choose some of them as more significant than others. In other words, the statistical investigation is possible only "if we know what is pertinent and what we would like to obtain more information about." Adorno has the merit of assuming straightforwardly this *explicit* typology that is his own; and that, he says, rests "upon the adequacy or inadequacy of the act of listening to that which is heard" (3). This is where the *presupposition*, affirmed and avowed, of the *work* intervenes:

> A *premise* is that works are objectively structured things and meaningful in themselves, things that invite analysis and can be perceived and experienced with different degrees of accuracy. What the types want . . . is to stake out realms of their own, realms that range from fully adequate listening, as it corresponds to the developed consciousness of the most advanced professional musicians, to a total lack of understanding and complete indifference to the material. (3; emphasis mine)

The work, the works: that seems to be for Adorno the only *objective* pole on which can be propped a sociology of musical listening that threatens otherwise to be lost in the elusive and infinite variety of *subjective* individual reactions. And, faced with this single objective possibility—to start from works—Adorno refuses to get involved with seemingly more "scientific" methods ("experimentation" recording "the literal, perhaps physiological and thus measurable, effects which a specific music exerts," such as "accelerated pulse rates" [4]) or the most currently "sociological" methods based on "verbalizing their own musical experiences," since the former cannot grasp "the esthetic experience of a work of art as such" (which is, we will readily agree, of a different order from simple stimulus-response), whereas, in the case of the latter, "verbal expression itself is already prefiltered and its value for a knowledge of primary reactions is thus doubly questionable." That is why, Adorno concludes, provided one can "grasp an attitude" (an attitude of listening), one must start with "the specific quality of the object," namely *the work*.

I will try to show you both the soundness, the necessity of Adorno's position, and its essential limitations, stemming from the fact that he places the work in the position of precisely an *object*. No doubt one can, one should, start from works. But they are not *objective data* by means of which one should measure the adequacy of a listening: for the very reason that works bring into play *competing listenings*, as you will see in Mozart's *Don Giovanni*, which we will listen to soon. There is no ideal way of listening to *Don Giovanni*, then (and more generally: to a work), since *this opera makes us hear several different listenings*. We listen to *some* listenings (characters, "types" listening)—which irremediably complicates Adorno's analysis.

Moreover, and even more seriously, we cannot say that the work is the objective pole of listening, since the history of the notion of the work *conditions* the history of listening, *and vice versa*. That there is a history of the notion of a work is not self-evident; but I hope I have convinced you that the seemingly obvious idea according to which *individual musical works exist* has emerged only slowly, in close correlation with the constitution of authors' rights and with the consolidation of certain practices of performance. That there is a history of *listening* seems even more *improbable*: if Adorno can write that "in many sectors of material sociology, we lack comparable and reliable research data on the past" (1), what can we say about listening? What could be the "reliable" traces of *actual* attitudes of listening, other than those provided by the "experimentations" Adorno speaks of (but they concern only our present) or by the "verbalization of their own musical experiences," which tells us nothing about listening *itself*?

My hypothesis here is that the history of arrangement—due to the fact that an arranger is a listener who signs and writes his listening—does indeed open up the possibility of a history of listening *in music*. I will come back to that. But let's look now briefly at what Adorno's typology consists of.

The "first type" is that of the "expert." He is defined by "entirely adequate hearing":

He would be the fully conscious listener who tends to miss nothing and at the same time, at each moment, accounts to himself for what he has heard. . . . Spontaneously following the course of music, even complicated music, he hears the sequence, hears past, present, and future moments together so that they crystallize into a meaningful context. Simultaneous complexities—in other words, a complicated harmony and polyphony—are separately and distinctly grasped by the expert.

The fully adequate mode of conduct might be called "structural hearing." (4–5)

Structural hearing: the expression is fertile. Here, as we see, it designates a form of *plenitude* that admits no void, no distraction, no *wavering* in listening, other than that of the brief comings-and-goings of memory between past, present, and future. It is a *functional* listening (it is *a function of the work*); it is a listening that, even though it *analyzes* (in order to grasp "simultaneous complexities . . . separately and distinctly") is finally aiming at a *synthesis*.

Despite some negations of Adorno's, the types that follow seem to be a *degraded* version or a progressive *degradation* of the first type:

Under the prevailing social conditions, making experts of all listeners would of course be an inhumanly utopian enterprise. . . . This is what bestows legitimacy on the type of the *good listener* as opposed to the expert. The good listener too hears beyond musical details, makes connections spontaneously, and judges for good reasons, not just by categories of prestige and by an arbitrary taste; but he is not, or not fully, aware of the technical and structural implications. Having unconsciously mastered its immanent logic, he understands music about the way we understand our own language even though virtually or wholly ignorant of its grammar and syntax. (5)

Now, according to Adorno, this type, as an intermediary type, tends to disappear and to be replaced by a "polarization toward the extremes" of typology until we have only the *expert* face-to-face with the representatives of an increasingly *fallen* listening, until music becomes pure "entertainment."[2] "The tendency today," writes Adorno, "is to understand everything or nothing."

What I would like to demonstrate is that this logic of *all or nothing* that Adorno thinks he can diagnose as a tendency in the recent history of listening is above all one that underlies his typology, and for good reason: it slips into it, surreptitiously but powerfully, thanks to the very presuppositions of *work*. Or more precisely: owing to a *particular* notion of the work. In other words, anticipating things somewhat greatly: with the notion of a work as Adorno presupposes it, we are *necessarily* led to this alternative: either to understand/hear *everything* (as it is, without arrangement being possible), or to understand/hear *nothing*.

Perhaps most surprising, especially if we ponder the fact that this typology is not mainly guided by concern for its statistical relevance, is the absence of one possibility, as "theoretical" and quantitatively insignificant as it may be: namely, that *distraction*, *lacunary* listening, might also be a means, an attitude, to make *sense of the work*; that a *certain* inattention, a certain *wavering* of listening, might also be a valid and fertile connection in *auditory interpretation at work*. Listening is not reading. But the comparison between the two can shed light on the surprise of which I speak. Reading a text, reading it in an "expert" way, we rewrite it, we draw quotations from it that are sometimes quite far apart from each other in the "body" of the text, we contrast and compare them, we make meanings and sometimes contradictions or paradoxes emerge from them that the linear structure of the text did not immediately make visible. One could even say that reading does not truly become *criticism* until it breaks with the temporal linearity of the stream. Until we render it discrete [*discrétiser*] by a certain *analysis*. What does this *critical condition* become in listening?—That, in brief, is the question that stays with us after we read Adorno.

It is with his typology still resonating, schematically outlined, and in the echo of this question, that I would now like to lend

an ear—but which one?—to a "work": *Don Giovanni*. All the
while keeping as a backdrop or stage curtain the two extreme
types of *structural listening* and *entertainment*.

"Listening, I Follow You" (Don Giovanni)

Mozart's *Don Giovanni* was performed for the first time in
Prague in 1787. The opera would be performed again the following year at the Burgtheater in Vienna (on May 7, 1788). Its success
in Prague was as complete as its welcome in Vienna was luke-
warm. For this difference in its reception, there are probably a
thousand contextual reasons. One of them (which we will return
to) might stem from the change that Vienna was in the process
of undergoing in its canons of musical listening. But there is also
a scene that Mozart and his librettist, Da Ponte, had explicitly
addressed to the Prague public. This scene, a veritable potpourri
(or "remix," as they'd say today), is an *arrangement* of opera
tunes recently performed in Prague. It interests us for several
reasons: first of all, because it portrays Don Juan and Leporello,
like two "disc jockeys" (DJs) before the letter, playing pop hits
for each other, repeating existing works in the key of *distraction*;
then, because it is a prelude to another scene (the penultimate)
where this *distracted listening* would not only be punished, but
especially be *compelled* to comply with the law of a serious, responsible listening, paying attention the whole time. Through
these two scenes in *Don Giovanni* there is a *certain* form of responsibility of listening that we will see outlined *in music*, shown
in a conflicting relationship with arrangement as principle of
dissolution. Faced with the listening we want to call the *wavering*
of Don-Juan-the-dissolute (I'll nickname him DJ here, his ini-
tials), the Commendatore will come to embody a recall to the
order of a *legitimate* listening. A structural one.

Scene 13 of act 2 reveals a room, a table set for a meal, and
some musicians. "Play, my dear friends," DJ sings; "as soon as I
spend my money, I want to be entertained" (*io mi voglio di-
vertir*). At which the musicians on stage play a few bars of *Una*

cosa rara, an opera by Martín y Soler to a libretto by Da Ponte, performed in Prague not long before the creation of *Don Giovanni*. Leporello *names* the piece: "Bravo! 'Cosa Rara.'" Then, while still supervising the service and bringing dishes, he announces the next piece on the musical menu: "*Vivano 'I Litiganti'!*," he exclaims, while the musicians play a few bars of a condensed arrangement of the hunting minuet from Giuseppe Sarti's opera *Fra i due litiganti il terzo gode*. As for DJ, he is eating. He tastes and comments on the dishes, implicitly grafting his culinary vocabulary onto that of musical taste, according to a traditional metaphor that becomes here doubly pertinent: the arrangements that follow each other in the manner of a potpourri belong to the tradition of "dinner music" (*Tafelmusik*); and, above all, they are in a way the musical symbol for DJ's *delectative*, or *dilettante* (from the Italian *dilettare*, "to take delight in") listening. The main course is well known: it is a self-quotation of Mozart, from his *Marriage of Figaro* (Figaro's famous aria, *Non più andrai*, at the end of act 1); it is a popular song taken from this opera that, not long before *Don Giovanni*, had enjoyed immense success in Prague. Leporello's commentary: "I know that one only too well!"

All these allusions, both nominal and musical, constitute a form of self-reflection in *Don Giovanni* on its context and genesis. But they also portray and summarize the *figure of listening* that is DJ, calling for or evoking works by their names and by *morceaux choisis* [selected snippets].

This charming family meal also prepares the way (it is even its prime dramatic function) for the entrance onto the stage of the Commendatore. This entrance is announced several times and delayed in the course of scene 14: after Donna Elvira, it is Leporello who goes to see the "thing" that stands at the threshold to the house and knocks. Cry of fear from Leporello and a question from DJ: "Leporello, what is it?"

This is where, in Leporello's reply, a rhythmic theme is heard that will take on increasing importance. Leporello mumbles, stammers, imitates the *footsteps* of the "stone man" who is approaching: "If you heard (*se sentiste*) the sound he makes, Ta ta ta ta. . . ." This *theme of the Footstep* (as the poet Pierre-Jean Jouve so aptly calls it), uttered in long, regular beats, imposes its *imprint* on Leporello's discourse. And right away it is associated with *listening* ("If you heard," *se sentiste* . . .), as are also the blows the Commendatore soon strikes on the door: "LEPO-RELLO.—Ah! Listen (*sentite*). DON GIOVANNI.—Someone is knocking. Open. . . ."

After the dissoluteness and distraction of the potpourri scene, these footsteps (along with their echo in the blows on the door) come *to recall listening to a structural memory*. For, when DJ goes to open the door himself to the statue (while Leporello hides under the table), not only does he open the door to a ghost who will hasten his punishment, but he also opens the music of the opera onto his own past, onto the harmonies and rhythm of the Overture. In other words: after the meanderings of the dilettante listening of the dinner music, the Commendatore comes to recall the law of a *structural listening*. Forcing the opening of the door with his footsteps and blows, he comes to remind us that an opera must remember its Overture; that, in order truly to conclude, the conclusions of a work, or an *opus* (singular of *opera* in Latin), must repeat its beginning, must loop the loop of its unfurling, must close the circle of its *compositional economy of listening*.

Scene 15 (the penultimate) gives this recollection the *force of law*. It is clear that, in his first words, the Commendatore is *returning* (he is a revenant) in order to sound a reminder of the *cadence* of the Overture. And, as Michel Noiray so aptly says, he does this "by nailing the name of his victim onto it."[3] It is this address with its unforgettable scansion—"Don Gio-*van*-ni . . ."—that inexorably imposes the trochaic, solemn rhythm of the Overture onto the *name* of DJ. Recalling him to order (and recalling us listeners along with him), to the law of a definite responsibility of listening.

Every promise, the Commendatore seems to be saying here, must be kept; there could be no *musical* disloyalty in the finale of an opera. At the cemetery (act 2, scene 11), the statue had promised to accept DJ's invitation ("Will you come to dinner? Yes."). A promise that it recalls in the beginning of scene 15: "Don Giovanni, you invited me to dine with you, and I have come." By this call to order of a promise given and kept, the Commendatore essentially interrupts the delectative drift of listening, he *stops* it: "Stop" (*ferma un po'*), he says gravely to DJ who is getting ready to serve him his meal; "he who has tasted heavenly food does not taste earthly food." But, in the end (after a complex exchange that produces a change in the system of listening), far from yielding to DJ's invitation, the Commendatore *invites* him, in turn, to yield to a certain *economic law* of listening, putting an end to the dilettante drift that after that seems essentially like a *waste of time*:

DON GIOVANNI: Speak, then: what do you want . . . ?
THE COMMENDATORE: I speak, listen: I have no more time [*Parlo, ascolta: più tempo non ho*].
DON GIOVANNI: Speak, speak: I'm listening to you [*ascoltando ti sto*].
THE COMMENDATORE: You invited me to dinner, you know now what your duty is. Answer me: will you yourself come to dine with me?

As this dialogue unfolds (complicated by Leporello's asides), it is time, then, that is counted once again, to put an end to the boundless expenditure of auditory distraction. To DJ who, in the beginning of scene 13, sang "As soon as I spend my money, I want to be entertained," the Commendatore recalls that there is no more time; or rather, that he must *answer* (answer *for the time that's passing and for the music that is passing by in it*), in short, that *the time of listening cannot be spent without being counted.* That is, one cannot delay indefinitely, by means of meanderings in the form of potpourris or trifling arrangements, the *return* to the *payoff* that the beginning of the work had *musically promised*, in terms of the *economy of the composition* (themes, motifs, harmonies . . .). And, in fact, time—after DJ has said "I am listening to you"—is as if *measured by footsteps* in the orchestra: everything stops, the race comes to an end, we hear only one note repeated in cadence . . .

The answer around which everything pivots, *the* answer that confirms the victory of one *regime of listening* over the other, is in fact DJ's answer when he says "*ascoltando ti sto.*" How can we translate these words of DJ's, so idiomatic in his language, Italian? How can we adapt them in "good" French, while keeping all the possible readings they contain? How, in a word or more than one word, can we *arrange* them into another language, to let them resound with the echo of their own future, from whatever in them *remained yet to be heard*? The translation that imposed itself on me—beyond the versions that are indeed correct but are dully ordinary, which we find pretty much everywhere ("I'm listening to you . . .")—is this, which I'll give you first as is, in all its linguistic abruptness: "Listening I follow you" [*Écoutant je te suis*].

By abusing (a tiny bit) French, we can also hear in this: "Listening [to you] I *am* yours."[4] But, this time by forcing Da Ponte's language, one could also begin to understand: "Listening [to you], I *follow* you," I follow your *footsteps*, your rhythm, your step, I submit myself to the law you dictate to me by posing it as a theme or a thesis. We have indeed misused the Italian, in order to make it say what it says and what the music (the orchestra) utters without really saying it. On the other hand, what no translation or adaptation can convey is the resonance of the Italian *stare*. This verb (here conjugated in the first person singular, *sto*) in fact conveys the *stop*, the *stance*, or the *stasis* of one who, up until this fateful sentence, has been fluidity itself: the inscribable flow of a musicality that, like wine or blood, pours out in waves.

Listening to you, DJ says to the Commendatore (and this time I am no longer translating), I am paying attention to you, I come to a stop. Stop! Your law is a judgment [*un arrêt*] stopping [*arrêtant*] my fate—my fate as a dissolute listener and, beyond me, the fate of all of you who are listening to me at this very moment.

On the edge of the modern regime of structural listening, of *economical listening*, *Don Giovanni* portrays this listening in the violence of its law, in the takeover by force it carries over other regimes—the dilettante regime, for example.

Polemology of Listening (Berlioz and the Art of the Claque)

Opera in Latin is the plural of *opus*, "work"; but *opera* (the dramatic-musical genre) comes in fact from the Italian *opera*, "work," and its plural is *opere*.

Don Giovanni is an opera. And this opera portrays the two extreme types in Adorno and makes them confront each other: structural listening and entertainment. Already for this very reason, *Don Giovanni* is not a *work* in the sense that Adorno gives to this notion in his typology; it is above all not a work according to the *function* that Adorno assigns to works, namely a certain objective norm by which one can measure the adequacy of *a* listening. According to the etymologies I've just mentioned to refocus them a little, *Don Giovanni* is rather *several works*; not one *opus*, but a few *opera*. First of all, because *Don Giovanni* includes several fragments from other operas, adapted or arranged for the occasion. And then, because *Don Giovanni* comprises *some* listenings, two at least: that of entertainment (the "dinner music"), which belongs to an era *previous* to the notion of work; and the structural listening that throughout the nineteenth century will grow to accompany the *consolidation* of this notion of the work. In this sense, *Don Giovanni* is not several works in one, joined together in *one* work; we'll say, playing on the ambiguity of the singular and the plural, that it is *the works* (understanding *opera* as the Latin plural of "work").

However, *Don Giovanni*, in its dramatic architecture, *tends* to be *a work*, to be unified *as one work* precisely to the extent that one type of listening wins out over the other. Or rather: to the extent that the structural listening *condemns* the other, makes it at the same time obsolete (outdated) and *forbidden*. In this sense, *Don Giovanni* is certainly part of the *emergence of the notion of the work*, a complex historical movement that implies at the same time—as you'll remember—a related change in the legal apparatus regulating musical practice, conditions of performance of music, and attitudes of listening.

We can get some idea how much the idea of the work, and the listening it involves, must have been *imposed*, obtained after a hard fight against secular habits, by reading Berlioz's account in his *Memoirs*, written in 1835.[5] Here Berlioz describes his own attitude of listening at the Paris Opéra, surrounded as he, the *expert* listener, was, by a "little club" of enthusiasts, or "good listeners," as Adorno would say:

> When we saw, by the title-page of the orchestral parts, that no change had been made in the opera, I went on with my lecture, singing the principal passages, explaining the instrumental devices to which certain effects were due, and so enlisting the sympathy and enthusiasm of the members of our little club beforehand. Our excitement caused a good deal of surprise among our neighbors in the pit, for the most part good country folks. (53)

Berlioz the expert knows the score by heart, then; he explains it and analyzes it in advance to the *limited* circle of his friends who are "good listeners," to the great surprise of the average public surrounding them. Although he is not holding in his hands a printed copy of the *work* (as occurs sometimes with certain music-lovers today), he has still brought the score with him; he has it on him, *in him. Before* hearing, *while watching*, the performance of the work:

The three taps . . . announced that the opera was about to begin. . . . We sat with beating hearts, silently awaiting the signal from Kreutzer or Valentino. When the overture had begun it was criminal to speak, beat time, or hum a bar. . . .

As I was intimately acquainted with every note of the score, the performers, if they were wise, played it as it was written; I would have died rather than allow the slightest liberty with the old masters to pass unnoticed. I had no notion of biding my time and coldly protesting in writing against such a crime—oh dear no!—I apostrophized the delinquents then and there in my loudest voice, and I can testify that no form of criticism goes so straight home as that. (54)

Berlioz the expert exercises at the opera not only a kind of close surveillance of his neighboring listeners (imposing an attentive silence on them), but he also and especially watches over the *conformity of the performance to the preexisting score.* He "despotically" (his word) exercises "active criticism" (56). And this seems to him singular and unusual enough to be recounted at length and in detail.

Although it already foreshadows modern fidelity to the work (what the Germans call *Werktreue*), Berlioz's attitude seems not only a minority view, but it also falls short of the *silent* respect that would generally be observed later on. For, when with his "club" of "good listeners" he expresses enthusiasm and approbation, Berlioz seems hardly to care at all about the totality of what is being performed:

Then you should have seen with what a frenzy of applause we greeted the passages which no one else noticed—a fine harmonic bass, a happy modulation, a right accent in a recitative, an expressive note in the oboe, etc. The Public took us for *claqueurs* out of work, whereas the real chief of the *claque*, who was only too well aware of the true state of affairs, and whose cunning combinations were deranged by our thunders of applause, looked as furious as Neptune. (56)

To understand something about the *politics of listening* that are in play here, you have to know what the (French) institution of the *claque* was. This, as Michael Walter explains in his "Social History of Opera in the Nineteenth Century,"[6] formed an "intermediary field" between the public and the performers of the Opéra. From the time the Paris Opéra was under the direction of Louis Véron (1831–35), the *claque* was in the hands of a certain Auguste Levasseur: who, in exchange for his services, received either cash (from the singers or from the composer) or free tickets (from the management or the artists), which he could then sell at a profit. All this was the subject of an explicit contract. Whoever bought a ticket from Levasseur was automatically a member of the *claque*. The *claqueurs* (as Berlioz calls them; in *The Art of Music and Other Essays* he speaks of "the system of paid applause") were supposed to applaud at Levasseur's command; not, however, according to the arbitrariness of chance, but according to an in-depth study that Levasseur had made of the score, by attending rehearsals regularly and having discussions with the theater director as well as the singers. Often, on the days before the premiere, Levasseur decided on his plan with Véron after analyzing the opera. On the evening of the premiere, the *claqueurs* came in before the public in order to be better and more strategically placed. And Levasseur, dressed as conspicuously as possible, gave the signs for the beginning, the duration, and the intensity of the applause. So he was transformed in a way into a conductor, the mirror or double of the other, directing the public as the conductor directed the musicians.

The public concert, ever since it came into being,[7] has been in effect a kind of mirror of listeners. It is not just a place to hear works. It is also a theater where the members of the public observe each other. And themselves. It is a space where we come to look at those who listen. Where we go to see people listening, or even to listen to people listening.

Listening to (oneself) listening is also making the work into a battlefield: a theater of operations of listening where various camps clash with each other. But this battlefield, this *polemical* space where people listen to themselves listening to each other, sometimes complacently, sometimes bossily—in short, this theater where listeners are exhibited is subjected to a movement of internalizing reappropriation, of which I could unearth a thousand proofs and testimonials for you. Beginning with Schumann, our critic-arranger who, in his works as well as in his articles published by the *Neue Zeitschrift für Musik*, portrays these "companions of David," the most well-known of whom are Eusebius and Florestan. In order, as he says, to "expose alternately different points of view on questions of art." When Schumann tallies up the works he has heard publicly, an account directed at his listener-readers, he gives voice to a variety of *Davidsbündler* who oppose each other.

You know as well as I do: it is precisely this way that, in the heart of our most intimate listening, the internalized voices and murmurs of the author and the *claqueurs*, the hissers, the critics and enthusiasts of all kinds, clash with each other in us, each one maneuvering for a cutting-up of the work that conforms to his interests or convictions. And that is why the theater of the *claque*, with all its art and all its refined strategies, has so much to tell us about the *polemology* that inhabits our inner ear.

I would like to read to you, to you who so often come to listen to me listening, the incredible *Memoirs* that I have just discovered. And that resound like a strange counterpoint to the *Memoirs* by Berlioz, that battling listener, militating to hear the work as written. Here is the title page (Paris, 1829):

Memoirs of a claqueur / containing the theory and practice of the art of successes / by Robert, / *Chevalier du Lustre, Commandeur de l'Ordre du Battoir*, affiliated member of several

Claque Societies, etc. / Edition published, edited, revised, and accompanied by Notes by an old Amateur . . .

This Robert speaks of a "science" of *claque*; and the teaching he receives in this new "profession" has all the characteristics of an *initiation* by a master: "Then, he gave me basic instructions on the science of cabals, and discoursed, like a skilled master, on all the different tactics capable of making plays succeed or fail; I learned from him in what circumstance one should applaud or hiss, cry or laugh, be quiet or shout out, sneeze or blow one's nose; finally he revealed for me the most secret mysteries of his profession" (15).

The leader of a *claque* being a clever tactician, an acute strategist, is a military metaphor that we find in other works on the claque. Such as this fabulous anonymous pamphlet from the beginning of the nineteenth century: "*The Art of the Claque*, or reflections of an expert *claqueur*, on its formation, its usefulness, its theory, and its tactics." The first chapter of this brief "treatise" (Paris, 1817) is entitled "On the Necessity of a Theory for This Commendable Art"; and it opens with a parallel to the military art that will soon become *the* structuring metaphor, strung out at great length, of this sixteen-page satire: "Many people have claimed that the art of the claque was purely manual: what a paradox! Might as well say that the art of war is only the art of making sword-thrusts" (3). Thus the brief chapter 3 is entirely devoted to "The Art of the Claque Compared to the Art of War."

Robert's *Memoirs*, published by the "old amateur" twelve years after this *Art of the Claque*, also makes reference to *strategies*, in a vocabulary that is also full of military expressions. Thus, when Robert, in chapter 6, quotes the "claquo-diplomatic instructions" that Mouchival, his master, confided in him, it is a matter of "brigades in the service of the Théâtre-Français" (34) as well as "maneuvers" to be carried out during the actors' exits "nicely graded according to the rank of each artist"; and, here too, the *claqueurs* are organized into a strict hierarchy: "it is enough to keep one's eye open to the leader who, having the watchword, makes all the proper signals, just like the telegraphic movements of the general" (35).

But the *Memoirs of a Claqueur* are unfortunately silent on the precise nature of the "notes" that Mouchival took in the course of rehearsals. The *claque* remains in the end an "oral" art, then, a tactile tactic without "writing," which the "old amateur" (the publisher of the *Memoirs*) himself regrets in a footnote:

> Sometimes manuscripts, on which the passages that should be applauded are indicated in the margins, are given to the leaders of the claque. By means of this, the *chevaliers du lustre* ["knights of the houselights," a term used for a *claqueur*] rehearse at home. The one who can read most fluently *acts as author*, and the others practice the handling of the bravos. . . . We regret that M. Robert did not devote a chapter to this part of his art. (312; emphasis mine)

After quarreling with Mouchival, Robert, who now no longer belonged to the *claqueurs* of the Théâtre-Français, entered "into negotiation for employment as head *claqueur* at the Royal Academy of Music" (67). And note 42 clarifies: "These services are sold from hand to hand, and are regarded as a property that is no less transferable than that of authors." This allusion to copyright and to the debates that agitated opinion on this subject at the beginning of the nineteenth century is not an isolated fact, nor is it a random remark. In fact, the *moral* voice, the *authorized* voice of the "old amateur" who edits and annotates Robert's *Memoirs*, makes itself both the spokesman for authors and their rights as well as an antagonist of the practice of *arrangement*. I have often stressed that this conjunction is systematic; but it is no less remarkable that it appears here in the margin of a text on the *claque*. It is in fact in the *countertext* formed by the notes that we find *jointly and severally* asserted: (1) the condemnation of all *organized autonomy* of attitudes of listening (even if the form of autonomy targeted here, the *claque*, is probably one of the most primitive); (2) the existence of a perpetual literary property; and (3) the prestige of the original over adaptation or arrangement.[8]

Ludwig van (1): Attention

You will have gathered that when Berlioz wants to embody the safeguarding of a *good listening*, faithful to the work, he seems essentially like a *counter-claqueur*. Whatever the case, whether it is a question of the seemingly spontaneous enthusiasm of Berlioz and his "club" or of the strategic and commercial institution of the *claque*, the attitude of silent, meditative listening is anything but dominant in the 1830s.

Further, it would be pointless to think that we can *date* the related emergence of the modern notion of the work and the practices of performance or listening that accompany it and correspond to it. Rather we should view this history, for which I have gathered scattered bits and pieces and various accounts, as a complex, stratified process, involving different *speeds of sedimentation* according to the place and the musical genre.

According to recent musical-sociological studies, then, it seems that the *correlative* notions of "serious music" (or "great music") and attentive listening (one would like to say: "great listening"), if they were not *born* in Vienna (how, in fact, can we *locate* the "birth" of a type of listening?), were nevertheless *configured and consolidated* there in an unprecedented way in the last years of the eighteenth century. Tia DeNora has recently retraced, in a remarkable historical "micrology," the emergence of the value of "greatness" in music, crystallized around the name of Beethoven.[9] This emergence (or this "construction"), in order to be understood, must be seen in the context of a distinct value of "pleasure" that generally characterized "the musical Europe of the end of the eighteenth century." And which gave way, very quickly (in the span of just twenty years or so), to the "serious" and the "scholarly." It is a little like our operatic scene in

Don Giovanni that is replayed, in the same years, on the "historic" stage (or the other way round). In twenty years, the Viennese listener has changed his face and his ears; he has renounced the figure of DJ wildly copying and diverting the music of others; listening, he will henceforth be *all hearing*, devoted to the law of the work, to its rhythm, to its *footstep* or *stride*.

The microhistory of this transformation includes the figure of a certain Baron Gottfried van Swieten. This man, who was a diplomat before settling in Vienna in 1777, resided in Berlin where, on one hand, the musical life of the court was essentially centered on the heritage of Bach and Handel, while on the other hand, the movement (originally literary) of *Sturm und Drang* had powerfully configured the notion of the "creative genius" in music. Van Swieten, then, imported to Vienna these two characteristic traits of German taste (especially the former: namely, the cult of a heritage of "ancient masters").

Van Swieten (and through him a part of the Viennese aristocracy) was thus one of the main actors in this *genesis of musical genius*, as testified by the 1796 edition of the musical *Who's Who* of the time, the *Jahrbuch der Tonkunst von Wien und Prag*: the baron, it said, "loves only what is *great* and *exalted*" (emphasis mine: two values imported from Germany); and, at the concert, it is from the "traits" of the baron, "not always easy to make out for the uninitiated," that "semi-connoisseurs" attempt to read "what one should think of the music being heard." Around Van Swieten, with unprecedented force, a rift is outlined, between, on one hand, the seriousness of the connoisseur exemplifying the value of "greatness," and, on the other, a certain casual listening that will be more and more perceived as irresponsible.

The emergence of the value of "greatness" in music is *indissociable* from what DeNora calls the "new conventions regulating musical listening in concert halls." And, in this matter too, Van Swieten was a "pioneer":

His attempts in fact foretell the measures taken and institutionalized later on pretty much everywhere to discipline audiences. . . . According to the composer Sigismund Neu-komm [a student of Haydn], Van Swieten "used all his influ-ence in favor of music, even to obtain silence and attention during musical performances. If one heard the slightest whis-per, His Excellency, always seated in the first row, solemnly got up and with all his haughtiness, turning towards the guilty party, looked him severely up and down." (58)

Silence, attention, greatness: all these characteristics—of *great music* and its *great listening*—were imported to Vienna at the end of the eighteenth century and consolidated around the figure of Beethoven in the beginning of the nineteenth. Now, this type of listening supposes, as I have said, an attitude of fidelity to the work [*Werktreue*], as much in the listener as in the interpreter: a loyalty or respect whose conditions seem to have been gathered together very early on in Berlin, before these values arrived in Vienna with Van Swieten.

After witnessing one of the possible scenes of the birth of at-tentive listening, there is a question that remains, persists, is am-plified and resounds in my ears, after our reading of Adorno: If we understand the historical necessity by which the notion of the work and a politics of listening that correspond to it are con-jointly imposed, isn't there something that is also lost in the battle as to the *possibility* of an *art of inattentive listening*? In other words: Are distracted listeners always and necessarily *deaf*, musically speaking? Isn't there *also* a share of deafness (perhaps greater than we might think) in the *plenitude*, even the *totality*, that structural listening summons?

Ludwig van (2): Deafness

To let the whole range of this uncertainty develop, let us con-tinue to follow the stratifications of our modern listening through the interpretation Wagner made of a famous deafness, the most legendary of all: that of Beethoven.

In the 1830s, the difficulties of Beethoven's scores were the subject of rival interpretations that all pivoted around his famous deafness. In his *Universal Biography of Musicians*, published in 1837, François-Joseph Fétis attributed to the weakening of Beethoven's memory of sounds certain characteristics—problematic ones, Fétis thought—of Beethoven's last works: "Repeats of the same thoughts were carried to excess; development of the subject he had chosen sometimes went so far as to ramble; melodic thinking became less clear."[10] Deafness here is on the side of certain countervalues that we have identified as being those of *arrangement*: mainly repetition (the "repeats") and distraction (or "rambling"). Similarly, Adolf Bernhard Marx, in his 1859 study of Beethoven,[11] attributes to "diseased auditory nerves" the forty-seven repetitions of the same motif in the second movement of the Quartet in F Major, op. 135: this "sonorous image," he says, is "brooding, droning, in the mind" of the Maestro because of the failure of his organ of hearing. Deafness and its droning are the ready-made *excuse* for the inadmissible: a certain *mechanicity* that risks letting "great listening" get *stuck* in one place.

For other exegetes, though, the deafness of the genius is inseparable from his originality. It is even the *condition* for it: it is this deafness that founds genius in its inner clairvoyance, in its *clairaudience*. Deaf, the genius is all the more *transparent to himself* when he closes himself off from the noise of the world. Even if some previous articles had already cleared the way for this thought, it is unquestionably Wagner who raised the deafness of the genius to the level of a *divinatory principle*. Wagner's reading of Beethoven is all the more unusual, though, since it *also* calls attention to a deafness that is blamed for the imperfections of the work, which then (as we will see) must be corrected. *Arranged.* The way Wagner handles and manipulates Beethoven's ear, all the tricks or tropes he makes it undergo, should make us pause: we will see outlined in it a twofold face of listening, the two sides of an eardrum that vibrates and trembles between *clairaudience* and *derangement*.

Wagner's exclamation, in his *Beethoven* written in 1870 to celebrate the hundredth anniversary of the Maestro's birth,[12] is famous:

A musician without hearing! Is a blind painter to be imagined?

But we have heard of a blind *Seer*. Like Tiresias, from whom the phenomenal world was withdrawn, and who, in its stead, discovered the basis of all phenomenality, the deaf Musician, undisturbed by the bustle of life, now heard only the harmonies of his soul, and spoke from its depths to that world which to him—had nothing more to say.

With these lines, Wagner has powerfully contributed to establishing the interpretation of deafness in *visionary* terms. The *clairaudience* of the now-deaf Beethoven indeed always allows us to explain the lack of comprehension his music produces; thus Wagner writes, "What could the eyes of men of the world who met him still perceive of him? Certainly nothing but misapprehensions." But this clairaudience also makes his music—the music of "all the works of the Maestro that . . . come from that divine era of his complete deafness"—into the instrument that could absolve the listener from all "guilt" [*Schuld*]. "Thus," Wagner adds, "these miraculous works preach repentance and penitence." The Wagnerian listener, listening to the deaf genius, is, so to speak, structurally in the wrong, guilty, and indebted to his works. Which, however, in their complete transparency *to themselves*, preserving and recording without any background noise the clairvoyant idea of the divine seer, promise him, the listener of the world of appearance, a kind of *redemption*. But at what price?

It seems that deafness, according to Wagner, is the exact obverse to *total listening*, totally subject to the structural law of the work. Listening *askew* here becomes, if not impossible, at least unpardonable *in law*. But since the equals sign that Wagner implicitly draws between deafness and total listening is reversible, we are right to wonder, in turn, if this total listening isn't precisely a form of deafness *on the part of the listener*. To listen without any wandering, without ever letting oneself be distracted by "the noises of life," is that still listening? Shouldn't listening welcome some *wavering* into its heart? Shouldn't a *responsible* listening (which can account for itself as well as *for* the work, rather than simply respond *to* an authoritative law) always be *wavering*?

If I summon here the expression "wavering listening," it is of course because I am thinking of Freud's famous phrase, a phrase that might basically be saying this: the sense of a discourse is not a *given* to be deciphered, but must be *constructed conjointly* by the one who utters it and by the one who listens to it. It obviously does not go without saying that this *psychoanalytic* listening can be translated into the vocabulary and practice of *musical* listening. We will simply note, leaving the parallel open, that Wagner, as a good reader of Schopenhauer, also anchors his thinking on listening in a *theory of dream*, but of a dream that, unlike the one Freud will speak of, essentially remains the fruit of a consciousness that is transparent to itself.[13]

Thus buttressed up by a scaffolding of *ad hoc* philosophical foundations, the *clairaudience* of Beethovenian deafness was promised a fine future. Wagner, however, barely three years after his *Beethoven*, would make an about-face in his opinions. This reversal is expressed in a text published in 1873 entitled "On Performing Beethoven's Ninth Symphony."[14] Here we find this phrase, so unexpected to all appearances: "There can be no doubt that Beethoven's deafness had the effect of blunting his aural image of the orchestra, to the extent that he was not clearly conscious of precisely those dynamic instrumental relationships" (99). Wagner writes this after having conducted the Ninth in the old theater of Bayreuth, on May 22, 1872, on the occasion of the placing of the first stone of "his" own Bayreuth, the *Festspielhaus*; and he says he "afterwards studied ways and means of remedying the evil as I saw it" (97).

So it is Wagner who would introduce variants, improvements, into the works of the clairvoyant genius. Wagner, in other words, transforms himself here into an *arranger*; and, in order to justify his alterations, he reverses the value of the deafness that he had glorified in the phrases we've seen already; he turns it into a *derangement.*

Some modifications will be justified by the evolution of instrument-making: the horns and trumpets, especially, had become chromatic since Beethoven's time, and we might not see any harm done to genius in alterations that confine themselves to letting the works profit from recent organological progress. Because these instruments, before the invention of valves, could not reliably play certain notes, Beethoven's scores include passages where their parts are *incomplete.* Thus Wagner cites the "terrifying fanfare" of wind instruments that opens the last movement of the Ninth: a fanfare in which the trumpets are only included in a fragmentary way, thus creating an absence of a rhythmic beat that, according to Wagner, "did not free the melodic line" (108). Here, then, it is only a matter of remedying a melodic incompleteness that "the master could not possibly have intended." Thus Wagner decides "to join the trumpets to the woodwind throughout the two opening deliveries of the fanfare" (108).

But Wagner went even further. Aiming for the "*restituo in integrum* of the composer's intentions," wanting to "rescue a melody from obscurity and misunderstanding," Wagner sometimes thinks he has to *rewrite* entire melodic sections. Thus he explains at great length the alterations he made to a certain *espressivo* passage in the first movement of the Ninth (bars 138–42). The instrument in question, this time, is the flute, which has not, unlike the brass, undergone drastic modifications in its fabrication. Or rather, beyond the flute, it is the virtual ear of the listener that demands rewriting: for it is perhaps *this ear that has changed its fabrication, even more radically than certain instruments.* And the various arrangements, Wagner's among others, have their place in this evolution or revolution of *auditory organology*.

But let's look more closely at what Wagner does to Beethoven, at the auricular surgery he performs on this part of his corpus that this *espressivo* passage comprises. "The flute," Wagner writes, "instantly attracts attention: the listener is bound to be confused if the melody it delivers is mishandled," since the flute is the "topmost instrument" of all the instruments in the orchestra, something that "in the course of time Beethoven appears to have completely disregarded" (110). In his years of deafness, Beethoven may have had melodic ideas that were more clairvoyant than those of anyone else, but he has forgotten to transmit them in a sufficiently understandable way to the ears of his listeners. So much so that it is up to Wagner to fill this chasm between the "organ of dream" of the deaf man and "men of the world" trapped in appearances; it is up to Wagner to help the latter cross the abyssal distance that has indeed made the visionary idea possible (by untangling it from the "noises of the world"), but that has prevented its *realistic* representation.

In fact, in the *espressivo* of the first movement of the Ninth, Beethoven "gives the theme to the first oboe," adding the flute to it to double certain notes of the theme in a higher pitch, thus "distracting attention from the lower instrument [i.e., the oboe]" (110). Wagner, then, is intent on remedying this "damaging effect," this "disturbing" defect. Note that the negligence of Beethoven's genius, though it is not attributable here to a constraint of instrument making, bears on a point very similar to that of the trumpets of the last movement: namely, the rupture, the interruption, the *dis-traction of a melodic trait* that *should have been* continuous, but that is cut up into pieces by the partial intervention of an instrument (the flute) monopolizing attention. "Who can claim," Wagner asks, "ever to have heard the melodic content of those bars *clearly brought out*?" (114; emphasis mine). Wagner's decision, faced with the melodic uncertainty of this passage, is to remove all ambiguities. In order to *let everything be heard in full daylight*.

But his solution could not be more unexpected. In fact, he goes for help, in order to *settle* the melodic truth, *to an arranger*. Here is one more arranger, then, *from whose arrangement* Beethoven's intention can be brought back to itself in all its transparent truth: "Liszt with his unique insight was the first to reveal it [the melodic content of this passage]—I refer to his superb piano arrangement of the symphony. Ignoring the flute's continuation of the oboe's theme, the effect of which is mainly disturbing, he gives the continuation to the oboe, thus preserving Beethoven's notation from any misunderstanding" (114). Surprising Wagner, who, as if despite himself, letting down his guard, begins to multiply the intermediaries, as if the original truth of a musical idea was above all not to be sought in the original, as if it could come only from a *medium* even more lucid than the divine seer himself . . .

By arranging Beethoven, even by looking for his truth in the arrangements of others, Wagner, despite or beyond his seeming reversal on the question of deafness and clairaudience, contributes to *recomposing listening* (to making a new ear, like the good instrument-maker of hearing that he is). That is to say, he sets up and establishes a *regime of listening* under which *the melodic idea no longer suffers from any discontinuity*. Thus Wagner asserts that it is "vitally important . . . that the melody—which . . . may often be presented only in its tiniest fragments—should *hold us in its grip*" (119; emphasis mine) [*nous captive avec continuité*, "captivate us with continuity"]. Thus all instruments are continually called on to *outline a continuous melody for the ear*: to impose on it *the total listening of a compositional thought finally restored to itself, in its entirety*. Beyond the superficial differences between the two Wagners (the one who writes *Beethoven* and the one who conducts Beethoven's Ninth), it is the latter who contributes *practically* to completing the theoretical work of the former. In the meantime, between the two, the figure of the arranger has nonetheless slipped in, as if underhandedly or smuggled in. But this is the better to make us forget him, the better to erase, in the rediscovered experience of the work *in integrum*, the critical force of arrangement, as well as its configuring and reconfiguring power, too, when it comes to listening.

Schoenberg: "To Hear Everything"

That is the path Schoenberg in his turn would take, when he set himself to the task of arranging (that is, orchestrating) Bach or Brahms. And when he turns himself into an arranger this way, it is still and always with the purpose of a kind of reform of listening: to contribute to *constructing*, to *fabricating*, this modern ear that he has bequeathed to us or grafted onto us. Here is how he meant us to listen, as listeners to his or others' music.

In effect, Schoenberg has signed some *great listenings* to works of the past. By making us listen to his listenings, he has written down our own. That is why, beyond even what he may have said or thought about them, he was a *maker of listening*. At once a ferryman and a builder. A maker of organs attuned to those musical organisms that are, according to him, the compositions.

Schoenberg rarely said anything about transcription or arrangement in general. We can find some views expressed here and there, though, including a letter written to the conductor Fritz Stiedry;[15] in it, Schoenberg justifies his instrumentation of a chorale prelude by Bach in the following terms: "Our 'sonorous demand' does not aim for coloration 'in good taste'; colors [instrumental timbres] rather have the objective of clarifying the unfurling of voices, which is very important in the contrapuntal fabric. . . . We need transparency so we can see clearly. . . . Therefore I think the right to transcription becomes a duty here." So it is a question, for Schoenberg, not only of validating his right [*Recht*] to arrangement, but of making this right into a sort of moral obligation [*Pflicht*]. More precisely: one no longer has the right to transcribe without *absolute necessity*, out of a simple "taste" (even if it is the best of "good taste"). Henceforth there must be the constraint of this demand that was already

Wagner's: the demand for "transparency." What *commands* one to transcribe is the *total* audibility that Bach's work requires.

That is also the argument given by Schoenberg when he explains the reasons that led him to orchestrate Brahms's G-Minor Piano Quartet: "My reasons: 1. I like the piece. 2. It is rarely played. 3. It is always very poorly played, for the better the pianist is, the louder he plays, so that you hear none of the strings. I wanted to hear everything, and I succeeded."[16] Here too it was a question of rewriting, of orchestrating in order *to hear everything.* Not to adapt or negotiate, but rather *to make the work absolutely transparent to listening.*

And the listening in question here is not that of a given listener, or of a category of listeners one has to *take into account*; it is rather *structural listening* in Adorno's sense—or even, beyond Adorno, a listening *without listener* in which *the work listens to itself.* For Schoenberg, as we know, couldn't care less about the expectations of our ears. His often-quoted reply to the conductor and composer Alexander Zemlinsky, concerning the "cuts" Zemlinsky had suggested in *Pelléas and Mélisande* for a concert in Prague, bears witness to this;[17] about the "concerns due to the listener," he declares: "I have as few for him as he has for me. I know only that he exists and that, to the extent that he is not 'indispensable' for acoustic reasons (since an empty hall does not resound well), he disturbs me."

Beyond the provocative tone, we hear an organicist concept of the work being strongly articulated here (where the work is a whole that doesn't allow any cuts)[18] and a regime of listening whose ultimate, ideal aim is the absorption or *resorption of the listener in the work.* A listener who is somewhat distracted, inattentive, who would skip over a few tracks daydreaming—such a listener could fall away like a dead limb. Useless. Bringing nothing to the great *corpus* of the work. This organicism, in the radical (or structural) tendency that Schoenberg gives it, forms the cornerstone of the *construction* of a modernist regime of listening. It no longer allows any arrangement of or with the work, especially not any cuts. Or rather, it allows only one function of arrangement: its function of *auditory organology*, the only one that can still justify it, that is to say, make it *necessary*. There is no more arrangement except arrangement that lives up to this *obligation*: to hear everything.

So we can understand that, faced with this regime of *total or structural listening* (whose establishment we have followed from Beethoven to Wagner and beyond), what Adorno called the "arbitrariness of the arranger" becomes inadmissible. We understand why, for Schoenberg as well as for Adorno, a Busoni seems like the representative of another era of listening, a kind of *ancien régime* under which it was still possible to *adapt conjointly listening to the work with the work to listening*. Where the work and "its" listening (this being henceforth precisely not *its own* throughout) were both constructed in reciprocal negotiations or arrangements.

It is not a question, for us, of *restoring* here this "ancien régime." It is rather a question of showing how the modern regime of musical listening not only secretes its own paradoxes and resistances, but also is confronted with other mutations—those of the *media* of music—that destabilize it and prevent its accomplishment. The question that has accompanied us implicitly has always been: isn't a *certain* distraction a condition that is just as necessary for an *active* listening as total, structural, and functional listening is?

EPILOGUE *Plastic Listening*

I look for my words, in silence.

I look, from among all those that float around my listenings, for *le bon mot*. The right word, the apt one, the one that will come to seize hold and pluck out of the musical flux what I want to tell you.

But there are a lot of words. As Michel Butor wrote so well, "Every musical work is surrounded by a verbal cloud." Those were his words, in 1971; the first words of a brief essay published under the title "Les mots dans la musique" ["Words in Music"], in the journal *Musique en jeu*. And that same year Butor constructed a little literary machine made of numbers of words, to navigate as he liked through a musical labyrinth, to insert into it his commentaries, what he called his "interventions" and his "glosses."

Thus he came to slip into Beethoven's *Diabelli Variations*, taking advantage of the pauses that articulate them, letting flow these words that asked nothing but to rush in. That is how his *Dialogue with 33 Variations by Ludwig van Beethoven on a Waltz by Diabelli* proceeds:[1] "opening wide" the pages of the score, enlarging "excessively" (his word) the silences that are there, in order to "house," as he says, a proliferating text. A guest who invited himself.

Listen. This is the genesis of this mechanism for reading and listening, as Henri Pousseur recorded it in the same issue of *Musique en jeu*. It has a lot to tell us about the place of words in musical listening. On their arbitrariness. And on mechanisms for listening of all kinds, starting with recording devices.

Butor's *Dialogue* was born in response to a proposition from Pousseur, who invited him to *comment on* the performance of Beethoven's op. 120 scheduled for Liège in September 1970. First letter from Butor on July 2, 1970: "Very difficult, really, to write a lecture on that in the usual sense of the word. I wondered if it might be possible to create a kind of dialogue, that is to say, *to insert the text into the variations*" (emphasis mine). Pousseur's commentary: "From that beginning there would develop, beneath my wondering eyes, a process of investigation and discovery, the invention and development of a host of structural, verbal, descriptive, and metaphoric methods, of a veritable *optical machine* capable of investigating Beethoven's universe and of 'revealing' (in the physicochemical sense) unnamed riches."

It is a question, in fact, of *naming*. Butor writes to Pousseur, on August 4, 1970: "To speak of the variations and especially to fix them in the mind of the listener, I am forced to give them names." There follows a "rough draft of nomenclature," which Butor foresees "will probably be greatly modified." Most of the variations, baptized "marches" or "waltzes," are simply *described*: there is "the light one," "the lively one," "the serious one," "the tender one," "the silent one," "the grave one," "the gentle one," "the slow one," "the contrasting one," "the murmuring one," "the singing one," "the pathetic one." Sometimes, these qualifiers are grouped so as to create larger ensembles: thus, "the light one," "the pleasant one," and "the lively one" (that is, variations 25–27) all form the series of "urgent" pieces. So that, already, other levels of naming appear, which emphasize the formal qualities of the cycle: the central variations (16 and 17) form what Butor calls "the pivot," variations 11 and 12 are called "incomplete," etc. Finally, certain appellations have to do with the musical techniques implemented ("the little fugue," "the big fugue," "the canon"), others with the intertextual relationships Beethoven's work has with what we call the repertoire.

Variation 22, in fact, takes its theme from Mozart's *Don Giovanni*. And Butor baptizes it simply "the quotation." That is self-evident. Yet this somehow minimal naming is far from being simply constative. It is even *performative*, since quotation in music occurs only with naming: naming *creates* the effect of quotation. Remember: John Oswald said that quotation marks do not exist in the "audio medium." But if the effect of quotation is to be something other than a simple, vague reminiscence, well, in order for *there to be* quotation *in effect*, there must be a gripping, arresting mark. After that, for lack of quotation marks, there must be a kind of *link* that both detaches from and refers to another context. When Butor grasps hold of a variation to call it "the quotation," he doesn't just describe a resemblance between musical motifs: *by calling it "the quotation," it is Butor himself who is in fact quoting.*

In Pousseur's words, we could say that Butor *reveals by calling it* the link between variation 22 and Mozart's *Don Giovanni*: he makes naming into a *revealing* use (in a sense that, and you will see why, I would like to call *photophonographic*). And *performative*, insofar as it transforms an auditory resemblance into an actual quotation.

On August 13, 1970, Butor writes to Pousseur that he was able to find "a recording" of the *Diabelli*, listening to which "has changed some perspectives": "The recording in particular drew my attention to certain very important *connections* that my first outlines violated. That is why I am sending you a new one, begging you to convey it to Marcelle [Mercenier, the performer scheduled for the concert-lecture in Liège], *with other names*, not yet all of them definitive of course, but already much more *revealing*" (emphasis mine).

So it is the *phonogram*, that is, the possibility of exact repetition, that at first reveals links, which in turn give rise to a new plan of revealing naming, itself provisional . . . Thus the "optical machine" functions, put to work by Butor to explore the "unnamed riches" of the *Diabelli*.

Letter dated August 23 to Pousseur: "Umph, I've managed to give birth to a still hazy draft of my dialogue. . . . Enclosed is my 'hyperprogrammatic' nomenclature with the place for interventions." So there is a new, final nomenclature before the concert-lecture, after which Butor will decide to "rewrite" his dialogue to make it into "a little book." And the interventions, grafts, commentaries, or glosses thus come to take their places between the variations, themselves in a way assigned to a nomenclature that Butor calls *hyperprogrammatic*. This word refers to that *program music* so disparaged by the supporters of a "pure" or "absolute" music.

We can never recall often enough that the term "absolute music" [*absolute Musik*] comes from Wagner, for whom it describes a non-motivated music, hence groundless [*haltlos*], having no *justification*.[2] This is the case, for Wagner, in Rossini's melodies, released or torn from [*losgerissen*] their foundation—language; but this is also the case in instrumental music that has been abstracted [*abstrahiert*] from its origin in dance. We must wait for Hanslick for this "absolute music" to become unarguably a positive value. So we can say, along with Carl Dahlhaus: "Historically, it is not the 'extramusical' that is added to absolute music, but on the contrary absolute music that constitutes a form of abstraction or reduction of types of instrumental music."

The power of Butor the listener is to accede completely to the programmatic dimension that continues to haunt *every musical work*, even the "purest." And, by complying with it, to aggravate it, make it proliferate, let it *overflow*. For—unlike so many musicologists who try to codify the laws of "musical signification"—Butor does not seek to limit meaning at all. With his words, he is not aiming to restore a "hidden program," a "narrativity" that underlies the work that must be *rediscovered*. He makes or lets *all* meanings proliferate. In all senses: semantic, graphic, optical, allegorical, literal, literary . . . That is why, somewhere in the *Dialogue*, Butor briefly explains his *hyperbolic* implantation of the process of naming: "In order the better to mark off our exploration, I have baptized the variations, but in order to respect the hyperprogrammatic dimension of the work, I have given each one *several names*; so we will see different arguments enumerated, closely linked to each other."

What Butor also attempts is to change the form of a musical flow, to cut it up in a different way: "If we wanted to change the prescribed order of the variations," he writes, and that is what he *does*. What allows him to *divide and increase* the cycle of the *Diabelli* are words and names; that is the surprising performative power of the naming machine he has built. It carries out this "great deployment" that "alone," for Butor, can give the work its "true dimension": it is this that *performs* this "expansion" of which the work, according to Butor, "dreams." This proliferating text that divides and increases the *Diabelli* by letting the variations get carried away, this *hyperprogram*, is thus a machine or a *program* to scrutinize the flow of music. It is a wonderful instrument for listening. Which makes the *arbitrariness* of signs into a truly *motivating* practice.

Ludwig van (4): The "Second Practice" of Track-Marks

It was probably such a *Diabelliciel* [a pun on *logiciel*, "software program"] that Roland Barthes was thinking of, also, when he listened to Beethoven. Not just to any Beethoven, but to the one he called the "second" Beethoven.[3] That is to say, the Beethoven of the *Great Fugue*, of the *Hammerklavier* sonata, or of the *Diabelli Variations* . . . But, by calling this Beethoven the "second" one, Barthes seems to have in mind a *second practice* of his music, more than a periodization of his works. A *seconda prattica*, then, not so much of Beethoven himself, but rather of his listeners. Thus the title of this essay by Barthes (*Musica practica*) is addressed above all to *us*, listeners of a new era of listening:

> The operation by which we can grasp this [second] Beethoven . . . can no longer be either performance or hearing, but reading. This is not to say that one has to sit with a Beethoven score and get from it an inner recital (which would still remain dependent on the old animistic fantasy); it means that, regardless of whether what is grasped [*saisie*] is abstract or sensual, one must put oneself in the position or, better, in the activity of a performer [*performateur*], who knows how to displace, assemble, combine, fit together; in a word (if it is not too worn out), who knows how to structure (very different from constructing or reconstructing in the classic sense). Just as the reading of the modern text (at least as it can be postulated, demanded) consists not in receiving, in knowing or in feeling that text, but in writing it anew, in traversing its writing with a fresh inscription, so too reading this Beethoven is *to operate* his music, to draw it (it is willing to be drawn) into an unknown *praxis*. (153 [translation slightly modified])

This new *practice* that Barthes and Butor (in different styles) seem to have glimpsed, this *praxis*, is potentially our own today. Butor's *hyperprogram*, like the performative or *operating* inscriptions of Barthes, is now within our reach, as extensions of our fingers. For, with the technical transformations presently underway in the digitalization of sound, our words become tools— variously scissors, hammers, or axes—to *touch music*. To touch works and their flow.

You read it as I do, every day, in the news: the near future of musical broadcasting and listening is being played out on networks of data communication, in the circulation of sound in the form of digital files. What this new commerce *of* and *with* music reserves for us, beyond the legal issues that are so often debated, is a *stock* of sonorous archives indexed and annotated with a view to their being *searched through* by search engines. Which are similar in every respect to the ones that consult billions of words, pages, and websites for us. Soon, I will be able not only to enter a few notes on a keyboard and immediately see unfurl at home a mass of recordings that contain them; but I will also be able (I can already, here and there) to type out on my keys a name, a keyword for a sound, for a work, for some passage or other . . . Which will immediately be sent to me. And which I in turn can send to you.

This is not a futuristic fiction: it is the reality that is being constructed all around us—there are a thousand proofs and tangible signs of it.

After the days of its analogical inscription, the digitalization of sound is today preparing the way for a new era of listening. And it is also a new *responsibility* of listening, which does not react solely to laws internal to the musical composition; it is no longer (no longer exclusively, no longer solely, if it ever was) structurally inscribed in the work or prescribed by it. For the digitalization of sound drastically changes *in fact* the criteria of listening as the works of music composed them. "Internal" determinations of listening (its conformity, its appropriateness to melodic, harmonic, rhythmic, or tonal categories of works "themselves") are thus sought out, shifted, moved around. The digitalization of sound and the fact of its being networked gives texts an unprecedented discriminating capacity for musical flux. Operations "external" to the musical (to so-called "pure" music) are now endowed with the ability to create signifying segments in the course of the music's flow.

Digitalizing sound is thus a form of equipment, an unusual *instrumentation* of (the organ of) listening. Generalizing what the history of Western music has called "arrangement" or "transcription," giving words the power to touch music (rather than describe it), it opens new possibilities for an effectiveness of listening, that is to say for its *immediately operative* quality; it allows music to be indexed, annotated, on a scale unknown until today. And this change of scale is not only quantitative; it is also qualitative, it may even touch music's mode of existence, for us.

This era of listening—there is nothing gratuitous about it—is also the era when listeners become authors. They are the DJs of today, who draw equally from *stocks* of analog or digital recordings (vinyl or compact discs). You can watch them writing numbers, words, indications of speed or order *onto* their disk tracks:[4] *onto the very surface* of the phonographic support, on the grooves where the sound is inscribed, they trace *track-marks*. They annotate, index, or comment in order, as Barthes would say, "to move, group together, combine, put together" music already in stock whose phonographic writing they overwrite with "a new inscription." To write anew, to *operate on* it, that is to say to *make a work*.

The DJs' inscriptions, their track-marks, are *operators*. In what Adorno called the "fine undulations" of the grooves on a disk, *on the very surface* of this mysterious tracing "which here and there forms more plastic figures,"[5] they engrave instructions that are their *allegros*, *a tempos*, and *da capos* . . . They inscribe signs, like us summoning music from our fingertips, with words. Their hand manipulating the disks resembles ours touching the keys of a keyboard. It resembles the hand that Adorno described in a wonderful little text entitled "Worte ohne Lieder": "The hand that strikes keys in the material," he said, "chisels" [*meißelt*]; and, after that, these words that "are formed plastically" are no longer read, "they let themselves be fingered [*abtasten*] again."[6]

This *plasticity* of words that Adorno speaks of here about old typewriters is also that of music under the organ of words-sounds that we have within our reach. *Worte ohne Lieder*, he said, "words without songs": as if words no longer expressed the soul of song, as if they no longer described, after the fact, affects given to our hearing in the flux of an internal voice (Barthes's "animism"); rather as if they analyzed, as if they moved around and segmented, in short, as if they *chiseled* music. *Plastically* and by *touching* it, by an arbitrariness that is immediately *pertinent*.

In this new *organology of our ears*, it becomes more difficult than ever to distinguish between *the organ* and *the instrument*. Thus, according to the Greek etymology of *organon*, the organology of which I speak is both that of our organs of listening that are most our own and closest to us—our pinnae and our eardrums—*and* that of all kinds of instruments, more or less mechanical or automatic, which assist our listenings. From the former to the latter, from organs to prostheses, and in their possible confusion, all of modernist thought on listening is brought into question. First of all in its *structural* postulate, which at bottom wants musical listening to be an internal matter. That is to say also *without any difficulties* ["sans histoire(s)," literally "without stories" and also "without history"].

I can hear you protesting but also agreeing. True, you whisper to me, the technical and social conditions in which we hear music have changed our listening; indeed, in this sense, there is a history of listening, with mutations, ruptures, changes of regime. But where you hesitate to follow me is when I say not only that listening is a matter of words (that's all right, others have said it before me),[7] but above all that it is a matter of *touching*. Long-distance or immediate touching, by networks or by manipulations, it matters little: listening *with our fingertips*, that is what you won't grant me without resistance. For—and this is just good sense—listening is not reading, especially not Braille reading. It is an *auricular* operation, not *digital*. We should not confuse organs and senses, or the organs of the senses. We would risk no longer understanding anything, no longer hearing. Being deaf.

Perhaps. Wait, listen.

I would like, before I go back to the distinctions between the senses, to talk to you one last time about the great deaf one. And about what happened to him for his birthday.

Ludwig van (5): The Prostheses of Authenticity

Mauricio Kagel has given us an excellent understanding of the plasticity of listening—its historicity, its deformations and conformations recording all kinds of mutations.

In fact it was the reception of Beethoven, of his genius and his *clairaudience*, that Kagel has portrayed as a person in *Ludwig van*, a film made in 1969 and released in June 1970, when the festivities of "Beethoven Year" were in full swing for the bicentenary of his birth. A hundred years after Wagner's *Beethoven*, in the centenaries of birthdays, comes Kagel's *Ludwig van*.

After a brief prologue, the camera identifies with the *point of view* of Beethoven "himself," who is returning to Bonn, the city where he was born. Getting off a train, he walks through the city, meets the surprised gazes of passersby, discovers the monuments that have been erected to him, and finds himself, before the windows of record shops, face-to-face with his name on the labels of recordings of his works. When he enters a record store and sees customers listening to his masterpieces with a headset before deciding to buy them, we, as spectator-listeners of the film, listen to the music from a *double point of listening*: it resounds, fading and far away, as if through earphones, but also as it sounded to the ears of the great deaf man. The film, which turns us into *clairvoyants* (by assigning us, by means of the camera's eye, the point of view of the Master "himself"), also, correlatively, makes us into *hearing-impaired* people. And Kagel makes this portrayal of the *point of listening* into the basis that allows us to explore *plasticity*.

For, beyond his most obvious "subject," namely Beethoven "himself," Kagel's film is also a series of variations on *plastic materials* of all kinds. The scene of the record shop is followed by a scene filmed in the press-molding factories where music's supports, magnetic tape and vinyl, are surveyed by the camera: we see their deformations, their impressions or the imprints they receive, their *molding* . . . But it is also the whole Beethoven-like imagery that becomes the subject of a *plastic* labor in *Ludwig van*. For the imaginary décor of the different rooms of the "Beethoven-house" [*Beethovenhaus*] in Bonn, which the Master (re)-visits under the supervision of a "guide," Kagel has appealed to *plastic artists*. In the bathtub designed by Dieter Rot float "heads of Beethoven," made of fat and glaze, deformed to the point of being unrecognizable. In the kitchen as conceived by Joseph Beuys, we discover all sorts of utensils, some of which (the funnels) evoke acoustic trumpets and other *prostheses for listening* that form one of the recurrent motifs in the film. There is also a mask that transforms the pianist Klaus Lindemann into Linda Klaudius-Mann, a kind of ageless ghost for a soiree-recital where he (she) interprets the *Waldstein* sonata.

This *generalized plasticity* that affects bodies, objects, faces, or supports is masterfully deployed in the inseparably visual and sonorous deformations portrayed in the "music room" scene. This *Musikzimmer*, conceived this time by Kagel himself, is a plastic work in a class of its own: all the furniture, all the objects, are covered with pieces of Beethoven's scores in a giant collage that, for the eye of the spectator, lets "no right angle" persist.[8] And the erasing of contours, the flattening of perspective—a result of Kagel's *plastic* work on written supports that existed previous to recording—also has its immediate *musical* counterpoint.

For if the whole soundtrack of the film is nothing but a vast *arrangement* of fragments of Beethoven (we hear in the beginning the scherzo from the Ninth resounding on electric guitar while the camera films a street musician), this soundtrack takes an unusual turn in the scene of the *Musikzimmer*: as the camera sweeps over the fragments of scores that cover the walls and the furniture, the spectator's eye establishes degrees of varying correlation between a notation glimpsed and a scrap of recognized theme. The scene is interrupted by a brief passage of the camera into the "storeroom" designed by Robert Filliou: the guide opens the door, and the scores that tumble out bear the names Liszt, Schoenberg . . . The guide gathers them up with difficulty: the history of music is weighty.

If Kagel makes us see the museification (the plastification) of musical genius from the point of view of Beethoven-the-revenant, he also makes us hear his music from his *point of listening*. That is to say, from his legendary (semi-)deafness. By design, by letting the camera ("Beethoven") leaf through the fragments of scores that form the "wallpaper" of the *Musikzimmer*, Kagel plays on effects of haziness, of faulty focus, or of *overexposure*. And he asks his musicians to take account of this by "deformations of instrumental tone."

However, Kagel's rereading of Beethoven does form a kind of *authenticity*. It even draws all its critical power from its eminently paradoxical nature: "The ideal thing," Kagel declares, "would be to interpret Beethoven as he heard (himself), that is, 'poorly.' That is what I tried to compose in my film *Ludwig van*."[9] Kagel thus assigns his "deformations" a place of authenticity even more authentic than that of a Harnoncourt: it is no longer simply a question of playing Beethoven with instruments of the era and according to the conventions of interpretation of his time, but of playing him *as he (did not) hear himself*. And from then on, it is this kind of authenticity doubled over on itself and taken literally that "restores" Beethoven's music to a form of *crudeness*, as Kagel said, that it had lost.

Kagel has thus *turned* authenticity *against itself*; he has made it a factor of deformation without precedent, while still portraying it as such. With him, authenticity (deafness as faithful and total listening) has become a *critical power* in which the appropriation of the arranger ends up in the most disturbing disappropriation. Perhaps we have now set foot outside a certain regime of listening, in favor of what Duchamp called an "ironicism of affirmation."

Hearing Listening: Summary of Listening(s)

At the end of a long journey that has led us straight from *law* to *listening*, I draw, from the little notes that Duchamp liked to arrange in boxes, the two that follow; they are abyssal:

1. "One can look at seeing; one cannot hear hearing."
2. "One can see looking. Can one hear listening, smell smelling, etc. . . . ?"[10]

A tiny—yet immense—space separates these two versions, which are almost identical and thirty years apart. Since their variations seem minimal, I am taking the risk of gathering them together and joining them under the term *reflexivity*: whereas the activity of the sense that is sight can take itself as object, whereas one can look at someone looking (another person, or oneself in a mirror), in short, whereas sight can thus be *reflexive* or *reflective*, it seems impossible to listen to someone listening. Common sense (but what sense?) would have it that someone listening doesn't make any sound; or else, if he does, it is only secondary (leaning over, for example, or moving around) and not *as a listener*. Listening *as such* is thus *silent*, it cannot be heard.

Now, this obviousness of common sense becomes complicated if we look more closely at the differences that our two notes present. Version 1 gives "hear hearing," a simple duplication of the same verb. While version 2 opts for two different verbs ("hear listening"), and also reverses the order of version 1: it is no longer "looking at seeing," but "seeing looking." What I hear in this chiasmus is the passive vs. active difference. Or rather: nonintentional vs. intentional. If *listening* [écouter] is not the same thing as *hearing* [entendre], if *looking* [regarder] is not *seeing* [voir], this is because we listen or look while *wanting* to perceive, intentionally; whereas one *hears* and *sees* even without wanting to.

Perhaps there is a possible explanation there for the shift, between version 1 and version 2, from *negation* (impossibility) to *question* (possibility that is open, hypothetical). "One cannot" / "Can one?": from one to the other, Duchamp seems to be saying: as soon as it is a matter of "hearing listening" rather than "hearing hearing," we are no longer sure of the impossible: *we must see*, perhaps, perhaps . . . Someone who *listens* with attention and intention, can that be heard? Do we ever know . . .

But, even if we thus *reduce*, by going from negation to question, the difference of senses (sight vs. hearing), we do not gloss over the problem—far from it. On the contrary, it seems that Duchamp, by looping or folding each sense *over itself*, affirms and consolidates the borders that isolate sight in its singularity: it is for sight alone that reflexivity *is beyond doubt.*

Whatever the case may be with sight and its privileges, the motive of the reflexivity of listening (hear hearing, listen to listening) has continued to accompany us. And we have done nothing, perhaps, but question its necessity and its conditions for possibility: by regularly posing the question of a *responsibility of listening,* we have tracked down the moments of this *reflexive return to self.*

To listen to oneself listening (if that were possible) would in fact be the first condition required to open something like a critical listening. But to listen to oneself listening, to fold listening onto itself and onto oneself, isn't that also risking not hearing anything anymore of what is available to be heard, isn't that *becoming deaf?* It is in the space of this risk that I ask you a few final questions: about the *responsibility of listening;* and about its *plasticity.*

To listen to oneself listening would be, probably, to stop hearing *totally.* But it is also because of this condition (of a rendering discrete [*discrétiser*] of listening, which has become incomplete or gapped to the very extent that it is reflective, that it is no longer all hearing, all attention) that listening that is inventive for today can be invented. It is, in any case, this improbable reflexivity that dogs my listening, that holds it in its attention. The listener I am is nothing, does not exist so long as you are not there. There or elsewhere, it doesn't matter, so long as my listening is addressed to you. The listener I am [*que je suis*] can happen only when I follow you [*je te suis*], when I pursue you. I could not listen without you, without this desire to listen to you listening to me, not being able, since I am unable to listen to me listening.

In sum, my question, for us, has been (hear it with all the chances, nuances, that our idiom preserves): *What summons us to listen?*

There is, of course, the work. It *demands* our listening, it *summons* us to hear it. But it asks us to hear it *plastically,* rather than according to one *type* of listening or another. Thus, *before* he is a dissolute listener rather than an expert one (before he enters one class or typology or another), Don Juan has been a *plastic* listener. Not (or not only) because he has picked out potpourris and arrangements of fashionable works, thus tasting elongation or compression, the elasticity of the popular tunes of his time; but also because, listening to the Commendatore, he has above all espoused a form, a figure of listening.

It is this plastic listening, which is also my plasticity as listener, that I experience when I listen to an arrangement of a work. For arrangers sign their listenings. We hear them hearing; and that is why, through the plastic ordeal they make the work undergo, we sometimes *believe we observe ourselves listening.*

Aside from the work, there is *also, inseparably given along with it,* our irrepressible desire to listen to listening. To the other. And the work is a work, that is to say it is *at work,* only so long as it *is still yet to come,* only to the extent of this desire that it opens. The work is a work, that is to say an event or experience *to undergo,* only when, beyond itself and its boundaries, it *leaves something to be desired.*

That is what, according to another range of this same word, *summons* us to listen. Lend your ear to this syntax that I misuse only slightly: what summons us to listen, what makes us into *two, one plus one,* what makes us into this open addition, this sum that we are [*cette somme que nous sommes*], is our desire for someone, always one more person, to hear us hearing. I want you to listen to me listening; and we want him or them to listen to us listening . . .

We are not a community of listeners listening to one single object that joins us together, like that population with mute ears that Wagner seemed to dream of. We are an infinite addition of singularities that each wants to make itself heard hearing. Thus without any possible summing up. We do not listen *like one single body*: we are *two,* and (therefore) always one more.

NOTES

Ascoltando

1. Just as I am writing these words, Peter Szendy himself discreetly reminds me that Don Giovanni sings "*ascoltando ti sto*"! There it is, then: the echo had preceded me . . .

2. Suzanne plays on these two senses in *The Marriage of Figaro* when she slaps Figaro instead of listening to him: "*senti cara!—senti questa!*"

3. Of course we must not ignore the fact that this immanent structure of layering or folding over [*pli ou repli*] belongs to every register of *sense*, once again in all the senses. There is nothing visible, of course, without its immanent reflection. But the sonorous is in a way the origin and presentation of this structure for itself.

4. I am referring here to the decisive studies by François Nicolas. Thus, in *La singularité Schoenberg* (Paris: IRCAM–L'Harmattan, 1997), 18: "In music, the true subject is the work, not the musician," an assertion that one should extend to every register of art, in keeping with the reminder in the previous note.

5. Ibid., 90.

6. "Listening" here would offer a differential in relation to and in the "presence-to-self" of the philosophical "voice," especially the Husserlian voice, as Derrida has analyzed it.

7. Narcissism of complacency—"he listens to himself speaking"—and narcissism of compassion—"he listens to himself too much." But we will see how, in a very precise way, Peter Szendy shifts "listen to oneself" to a "listen to oneself listening" that does not answer to any of these schemes.

8. It would be captivating to study the differences and resemblances between musical "synthesis" and visual "synthesis": how the latter more obviously refers, at least at first glance, to the recomposition of already given forms, while the former seems more to extract new minerals from its machines.

9. In many respects, it seems to me (and if I dare speak from the depths of my incompetence), jazz has definitely constituted the first clear-cut emergence of a music ostensibly made to listen to itself in this sense: as much with respect to its social provenance as to its uniquely musical functions, jazz is stretched, or it will have been, towards its own assertion always still to come [à venir], always yet to be invented, and always disconcerting. I would readily say about jazz as a whole what Jean-Pierre Moussaron, who knew what he was about, writes about Helen Merrill and Stan Getz: "Starting from the perpetual de-centering of the conversations they're having with each other, the being-together of their song emerges in the proximity of what does not stop arriving." *Feu le free?* (Paris: Belin, 1990), 126.

"I'm Listening" (Prelude and Address)

Epigraph. Roland Barthes, "Écoute" (1976), in *L'obvie et l'obtus* (Paris: Seuil, 1982), 217.

1. As I write these lines, I come by chance—one example among so many others—on the program for the Strasbourg Philharmonic Orchestra for the 1999–2000 season; on the last page, I read: "For the comfort and serenity of all, we thank you to observe silence during the concerts and—especially—between the movements of the works. The use of cell phones is strictly forbidden."

2. We will see in chapter 3 the conclusions that Schoenberg will draw from this regarding Wagner's *legacy*.

3. I am purposefully borrowing these categories from Pierre Boulez (*Jalons* [Paris: Bourgois, 1989]), who has unquestionably been one of the great thinkers concerned with the structural, *internal* listening of music.

Chapter 1: Author's Rights, Listener's Rights (Journal of Our Ancestors)

1. The scene is reproduced in the famous study by Raymond Klibansky, Erwin Panofsky, and Fritz Saxl, *Saturn and Melancholy* (New

York: Basic Books, 1964). On "ringing" as a melancholic symptom, see the remarks by Giorgio Agamben in *Stanze* (Paris: Rivages, 1998), 35 (translated by Ronald L. Martinez as *Stanzas: Word and Phantasm in Western Culture*, [Minneapolis: University of Minnesota Press, 1992]).

2. French translation by Pierre Maréchaux (Paris: Rivages, 1995).

3. Adorno, "Anweisungen zum Hören neuer Musik," *Der getreue Korrepetitor* (Frankfurt: Suhrkamp, 1976), 188–248.

4. 465 BCE. See Annie Bélis, *Les musiciens dans l'Antiquité* (Paris: Hachette, 1999), 163.

5. Martial *Epigrams* 1.52. Cf. Augustin-Charles Renouard, *Traité des droits d'auteurs, dans la littérature, les sciences et les beaux-arts* (Paris: Jules Renouard, 1838), 1:16. The word *plagium*, originally, did not designate literary plagiarism, but the act of dealing in *people*, especially through sale. Various laws (to which Justinian's *Digests* and *Codex*, among others, bear witness) thus punished the stealers of children, slaves, or free men.

6. Quoted in Hansjörg Pohlmann, *Die Frühgeschichte des musikalischen Urheberrechts* (Kassel: Bärenreiter, 1962), 39–40.

7. Ibid., 87ff.

8. Carl Dahlhaus, *The Idea of Absolute Music*, trans. Roger Lustig (Chicago: University of Chicago Press, 1989), 55.

9. Friedrich Wilhelm Marpurg, *Historisch-Kritische Beyträge zur Aufnahme der Musik* (Berlin, 1757); quoted in Pohlmann, *Frühgeschichte*, 95.

10. *Gazette des tribunaux*, August 9, 1834. Quoted in Christian Sprang, *Grand Opéra vor Gericht* (Baden-Baden: Nomos, 1993), by far the best study on musicians' law in the nineteenth century.

11. See Hermann Danuser, "Auktoriale Aufführungstradition," *Musica* (July–August 1988): 348ff.

12. See John Small, "J. C. Bach Goes to Law," *The Musical Times* (September 1985): 526–29.

13. See Mark Rose, *Authors and Owners: The Invention of Copyright* (Cambridge, Mass.: Harvard University Press, 1993).

14. See Paul Olagnier, *Le droit d'auteur* (Paris: Librairie générale de droit et de jurisprudence, 1934) 1:176–79, which quoted a royal ruling of 1697 concerning the relations of "Messrs. the Authors with the Actors of the King": "Monsieur the Author will dispose of the

Roles of his Play as he wishes, following the Characters of each, as he has always done; And the Actors will comply with his intention." See also the *Traité de la legislation des théâtres* by Vivien and Blanc, published in Paris in 1830: the author "must attend the rehearsals; he can give the actors whatever advice seems fitting to him, order changes by which the staging would show him to a better advantage, and, on all these points, his opinions must be followed. Whatever concerns the performance of his work, the means to produce it, the interpretation of his thoughts, belong to him by rights; that is his innermost right."

15. See Sprang, *Grand Opéra*, 178ff.
16. Hector Berlioz, *Memoirs*, trans. Ernest Newman (New York: Dover, 1960), 344–45.
17. This is what is testified by an affair in 1824 involving Rossini and his French publisher, a certain Troupenas (see Sprang, *Grand Opéra*, 41ff.). He had acquired, to the great displeasure of other publishers, exclusive rights to the composer's works for France. Troupenas' disappointed rivals, especially Camille Pleyel and Antonin-Joseph Aulagnier, nevertheless published, in the context of the success of *The Siege of Corinth*, all kinds of "fantasies," "mélanges," and other "quadrilles" beginning with "the prettiest motifs of Mohammed, insertted (*sic*) into the Siege of Corinth." This kind of arrangement, essentially made for dance, had immense public success. Troupenas, fearing he would lose a large part of the benefits that his dearly acquired exclusivity promised him, attempted to bring suit against his rivals, accusing them of counterfeiting. Counterfeiting, in French law, is an *economic* harm done to the author or to his legal heirs by illicit competition. But in the Rossini affair, the courts were of the opinion that no wrong had been done to Troupenas, since he himself had not published any "fantasy" or any "quadrille" on *The Siege of Corinth*. The arrangements of this opera, *since they did not figure on the same terrain as it*, could not truly be regarded as competitive. So Troupenas was forced to bear the expenses of the trial and to pay damages to the accused.
18. See Sprang, *Grand Opéra*, 120ff.
19. See note 17.
20. See especially the knowledgeable entry, "Rossini," in the *New Grove Dictionary of Music and Musicians*.

Chapter 2: Writing Our Listenings: Arrangement, Translation, Criticism

1. In Leopold Stokowski, with the Philadelphia Orchestra, *Bach Transcriptions*, compact disc, Pearl, 1994.
2. Which is not in the least dishonorable or "sacrilegious," quite the contrary: everything I could say about the arrangement and a certain *plasticity* of the music should also be regarded in the context of the reading that Eisenstein suggests, called "plasmaticity" and elasticity of bodies, in the wonderful collection *Eisenstein on Disney*, trans. Alan Upchurch (London: Methuen, 1988).
3. See the 1927 facsimile edition published by Martin Breslauer Verlag.
4. See chapter 2 of Carl Dahlhaus, *Musikästhetik* (Cologne: Musikverlag Hans Gerig, 1967); and Lydia Goehr, *The Imaginary Museum of Musical Works* (New York: Oxford University Press, 1992), 116ff.
5. Charles Burney, *Dr. Burney's Musical Tours in Europe, Vol. II: An Eighteenth-Century Musical Tour in Central Europe and the Netherlands*, ed. Percy Scholes (London: Oxford University Press, 1959), 207.
6. Hector Berlioz, "The Musical Customs of China," in *The Art of Music and Other Essays*, trans. Elizabeth Csicsery-Rónay (Bloomington: Indiana University Press, 1994), 178.
7. *Mémoires d'Hector Berlioz*, ed. Pierre Citron (Paris: Flammarion, 1991), 97, 358, and passim.
8. "Sixth Letter," in Franz Liszt, *Pages romantiques*, ed. Jean Chantavoine (Paris: Éditions d'Aujourd'hui, 1912), 187.
9. Quoted in Michael Walter, "Die Oper ist ein Irrenhaus," in *Sozialgeschichte der Oper im 19. Jahrhundert* (Stuttgart: Metzler, 1997), 232.
10. We could cite a parallel here to the practice of cinema where, unlike in the theater, the actor does not embody a character liable to be continually reincarnated (Oedipus, Hamlet, etc.), but a role for which he is already the *type*. Film, after that, comes under the jurisdiction of the *remake*: "A film," writes Peter Greenaway, "cannot be re-worked, it can only be re-made." *The Stairs* (London: Merrell Holberton, 1994), 4.
11. Quoted in Walter, "Die Oper ist ein Irrenhaus," 235.
12. Franz Liszt, "De la situation des artistes et de leur condition dans la société" (1835), in *Pages romantiques*, 71–72.
13. Antoine Berman, *La traduction et la lettre ou l'auberge du lointain* (Paris: Seuil, 1999), 49.

14. Momigny writes: "The best way to make the true expression known to my readers was to join words to it"; or again: "The feelings expressed by the composer were those of a mistress who is on the point of being abandoned." On the grafting of a monologue by Hamlet onto the Fantasia in C Minor by C. P. E. Bach by Wilhelm von Gerstenberg, see Georg Schünemann, *Bach-Jahrbuch* (Berlin: Evangelische Verlagsanstalt, 1916), 24. On Beethoven and the *parolisation* of his symphonies, see Helmut Loos, "Zur Textierung Beethovenscher Instrumentalwerke," in *Beethoven und die Nachwelt*, ed. Helmut Loos (Bonn: Beethovenhaus, 1986).

15. André Madrignac and Danièle Pistone, *Le chant grégorien* (Paris: Champion, 1988), 42.

16. Colley Cibber (1671–1757), Poet Laureate and director of the Drury Lane theater in London, watered down Shakespeare's plays.

17. "Lettre III—À M. Adolphe Pictet," in *Lettres d'un bachelier ès musique* (Paris: Le Castor astral, 1991); emphasis mine.

18. Hanslick, *Du beau dans la musique* (Paris: Bourgois, 1986), 97; emphasis mine.

19. Ibid., 93–94; emphasis mine.

20. Paul de Man does not contradict this in the seminar he devoted to the famous essay by Walter Benjamin, "The Task of the Translator" (see "'Conclusions': Walter Benjamin's 'The Task of the Translator,'" in *The Resistance to Theory*, [Minneapolis: University of Minnesota Press, 1986], 80).

21. Letter 128. I say "seemingly" since we would also have to analyze the complex system of utterance in the *Persian Letters*; and the words that are generally attributed to Montesquieu—the condemnation of translation, pure and simple—would certainly not emerge unscathed. Who, in fact, is speaking in this dialogue? And above all, *in what language*? What implicit movements of translation traverse this *Persian* letter whose (fictive) author transcribes a dialogue heard *in French* in Paris?

22. Walter Benjamin, "The Task of the Translator," in *Illuminations*, ed. Hannah Arendt, trans. Harry Zohn (New York: Schocken Books, 1969), 81.

23. De Man, "'Conclusions,'" 82.

24. Especially that of the Aeolian harp, evoked when Benjamin mentions Hölderlin's translations of Sophocles ("The Task of the Translator," 81).

25. See *Lettres d'un bachelier ès musique*.

26. Brendel, "Où le piano devient orchestre. Les arrangements et para-phrases de Liszt," in *Réflexions faites* (Paris: Buchet/Chastel, 1979), 152–53.

27. Especially measure 21.

28. Measure 72. Instead of the octave interval (*fa-fa*) of the first version, the left hand must cover an interval of a tenth.

29. At measures 21, 68, and 72 of the *Pastoral,* the lower-register sections (cellos and double basses) are arranged according to a rhythmic superimposition that was singularly complex for Beetho-ven's time: on the same fragment in the F-major scale, the cellos play five notes (a quintole) and the double basses four (sixteenth notes). From this superimposition (five against four), a complica-tion of rhythm results that gives rise to a complex sonority: it gives the effect that a *shaking camera* does in photography. Whence we hear a *noise*, an effect of *timbre*, that we interpret as a *sonorous painting* of the rumbling of thunder (according to the indications Beethoven's titles give for the movements of this "program" sym-phony). No pianist's left hand could play this complex superimposi-tion by itself.

30. Quoted by Osamu Tomori in the *Cahiers F. Schubert* 11 (October 1997): 43–44.

31. Schumann, "H. Berlioz, 'Symphonie fantastique' (Op. 14)," in *Sur les musiciens*, trans. Henry de Curzon (Paris: Stock, 1979).

32. Robert Schumann, *Schriften über Musik und Musiker*, ed. Josef Häusler (Stuttgart: Reclam, 1982), 101 [French translation modified (233)].

33. See Richard Wagner, *The Art-Work of the Future and Other Works*, trans. William Ashton Ellis (Lincoln: University of Nebraska Press, 1993).

34. On this "early romanticism," see Philippe Lacoue-Labarthe and Jean-Luc Nancy, *L'absolu littéraire* (Paris: Seuil, 1978); English trans-lation by Philip Barnard and Cheryl Lester, *The Literary Absolute: The Theory of Literature in German Romanticism* (Albany: SUNY Press, 1988). See also Antoine Berman, *L'épreuve de l'étranger* (Paris: Gallimard, 1984); English translation by S. Heyvaert, *The Experience of the Foreign* (Albany: SUNY Press, 1992).

35. "Wert der Bearbeitung," in *Von der Einheit der Musik. Verstreute Aufzeichnungen* (Berlin: Max Hesses Verlag, 1922). I provide a translation of this text in *Arrangements, dérangements* (Paris: Ircam–L'Harmattan, 2000).

36. Cf. the extraordinary correspondence collected in *Correspondances, textes* (Geneva: Contrechamps, 1995); especially the letter from Schoenberg on August 24, 1909, in reply to Busoni, who had offered to publish the two versions *side by side*: "It is truly impossible for me to publish my piece with, next to it, an arrangement that shows how I could have done it *better*. That would show, then, that my composition is *imperfect*. . . . In that case, I would have either to destroy my piece or *rework it myself*." We are far from Schumann's idea of the *perfectability* of works, and arrangement has become an exclusively *authorial* affair (or *autocorrection*). (I have analyzed the arrangement of op. 11, no. 2 by Busoni in "Bref Schoenberg," in *La liaison*, ed. Bertrand Rougé [Pau: Presses universitaires de Pau, 2000].)

37. Adorno, "Zur Problem der Reproduktion" (1925), in *Musikalische Schriften VI* (Frankfurt: Suhrkamp, 1984), 442–43 [French translation by Szendy].

38. Berg, *Écrits* (Paris: Bourgois, 1985), 24ff.

39. Reich, "Re-Schoenberg," in *Arnold Schoenberg* (Paris: Théâtre musical du Châtelet, 1995). See also, in the same vein (although with weightier ideological presuppositions), the recent *Requiem pour une avant-garde* by Benoît Duteurtre. In *National Hebdo*, the newspaper of the extreme right in France, close to Jean-Marie Le Pen, Duteurtre's book was reviewed and "dodecaphonic" music was characterized as "totalitarian"; a "Communist" totalitarianism, obviously, since it grants "equal rights" to the twelve tones!

Chapter 3: Our Instruments for Listening Before the Law (Second Journal Entry)

1. Cf. Bernard Stiegler, "Programmes de l'improbable, court-circuits de l'inouï," in *InHarmoniques* 1 (Paris: Ircam-Bourgois, 1986), 126: "When he was twenty, [Parker] carried *two musical instruments* on his early tours: his saxophone and his phonograph—as well as records by Lester Young."

2. Walter Benjamin, "The Work of Art in the Age of Mechanical Reproduction," in *Illuminations*, ed. Hannah Arendt, trans. Harry Zohn (New York: Schocken Books, 1969), 221.

3. Béla Bartók, "Mechanical Music" (1937); I give a French translation of this text in *Instruments* (*Les Cahiers de l'Ircam 7*).

4. Rodolphe Burger, "Loop," *Revue de littérature générale* 1 (Paris: POL, 1995).

5. Adorno, "Du fétichisme en musique et de la regression de l'audition," trans. Marc Jimenez, *InHarmoniques* 3 (Paris: Ircam–Bourgois, 1988).

6. Quoted in Sprang, *Grand Opéra vor Gericht* (Baden-Baden: Nomos, 1993), 238.

7. I give a general outline of this history in "De la harpe éolienne à la toile," in *Membres fantômes. Des corps musiciens* (Paris: Minuit, 2002); English translation forthcoming.

8. *La Tonotechnie ou l'art de noter les cylindres . . . par le père Engramelle, religieux augustin de la Reine Marguerite* ["Tonotechnia, or the art of notating on cylinders . . . by Father Engramelle, Augustine friar of Queen Marguerite"].

9. Quoted in Sprang, *Grand Opéra*, 243, from which I am borrowing the details of the affair.

10. In the sense of the *right to publish* [*droit d'éditer*] that the revolutionary decree of July 19–24, 1793, allocated to the author: "The authors of writings of all kinds, composers of music, painters, and sketch artists who engrave paintings or drawings, will enjoy, during their entire life, the exclusive right to sell, have sold, or distribute their works in territory of the Republic and to transfer the ownership of it in whole or in part." This decree constitutes the counterpart to that of 1791, establishing a *right of representation*.

11. Cf. Georges Sbriglia, *L'exploitation des oeuvres musicales par les instruments de musique mécaniques* (Paris: Arthur Rousseau Éditeur, 1907), 29, from which I have taken all the following citations.

12. The law of November 10, 1917, "rescinding the law of May 16, 1866," is quoted in Philippe Parès, *Histoire du droit de reproduction mécanique* (Paris: La Compagnie du Livre, 1953), 23–24.

13. Adorno, *Essays on Music*, trans. Susan H. Gillespie (Berkeley and Los Angeles: University of California Press, 2002), 277.

14. The Greek *eidos*, or *idea*, as has often been stressed, refers to sight.

15. See Andre Millard, *America on Record: A History of Recorded Sound* (Cambridge, UK: Cambridge University Press, 1995), 25.

16. See Parès, *Histoire du droit*, 34ff., as well as for the following quotations.

17. The ruling of the Court of Appeal was very explicit in this regard: "Considering that in fact records or cylinders . . . receive a graphic notation of words pronounced, that the thinking of the author interpreted is as if materialized on it in multiple grooves, and then reproduced in thousands of copies . . . and distributed outside with a writing that may indeed be special but that may be legible tomorrow to the eyes . . . that, thanks to this repetition of printed words, the intelligence of the listener is penetrated with the literary work through hearing, as it would have been with a book through sight, or with the Braille method through touch; that, henceforth, it is a mode of publication perfected by performance . . . and that the rules of counterfeiting are applicable to it. . . . Considering that we could not object to the law of May 16, 1866 . . . that in fact this text, in its explicit terms, aims only at 'musical airs' and not at words; [the court] rules that the inscription on records or cylinders of phonographs or gramophones of literary works without song or else accompanied by music . . . is an infringement of the monopoly of commercial exploitation of the authors and their agents; Rules, on the contrary, that there is no counterfeiting in the phonographic edition *sui generis* of musical airs, without words."

18. Parès, *Histoire du droit*, 55ff.

19. Sbriglia, *L'exploitation des oeuvres musicales* 112 ff., as well as for the quotations that follow.

20. André Lange, *Stratégies de la musique* (Brussels: Mardaga, 1986), 117.

21. Parès, *Histoire du droit*, 26ff. During the conference dedicated to revising the Berne Convention, which took place in Berlin in 1908, it was admitted that "authors of musical works have the exclusive right to authorize the adaptation of their works and their public performance by means of instruments serving to reproduce them mechanically." This revision put an end once and for all to the freer arrangements that had prevailed since 1866.

22. See Igor Stravinsky, *Correspondence*, vol. 2 (New York: Knopf, 1984), 219.

23. He sold the rights for this new version to the Chester publishing house. This resulted in a dispute involving Chester and the Jurgenson firm in Leipzig. Chester lost the trial and threatened to turn against Stravinsky, accusing him of having sold what he did not possess.

24. See Eric Walter White, *Stravinsky* (Berkeley and Los Angeles: University of California Press, 1966), 154, as well as Louis Andriessen and Elmer Schönberger, *The Apollonian Clockwork: On Stravinsky* (New York: Oxford University Press, 1989), 32.

25. Schoenberg, "Igor Stravinsky, le restaurateur," in *Le style et l'idée* (Paris: Buchet/Chastel, 1977).

26. Igor Stravinsky and Robert Craft, *Expositions and Developments* (New York: Doubleday, 1962), 166.

27. Schoenberg, *Stil und Gedanke* (Frankfurt: Fischer, 1976), 390–91.

28. Schoenberg, *Style and Idea*, ed. Leonard Stein, trans. Leo Black (London: Faber & Faber, 1975), 371ff.

29. See Michel Gautreau, *La musique et les musiciens en droit privé français* (Paris: PUF, 1970), 318ff. Furtwängler had recorded for the radio broadcasting organization of the Third Reich. After Berlin was captured by the Allies, Soviet authorities seized hold of Furtwängler's recordings, then released them to authorities in East Germany, which in turn yielded them by contract on November 5, 1952, to Urania Records in New York. This firm then produced a record with Beethoven's Third, distributed in France by the company Thalia. Furtwängler died in 1954 and his legal successors served subpoenas on the American and French companies. The ruling of January 4, 1964, speaks of "violation of the rights of the artist over the *work* his interpretation constitutes." After the passage of the law of July 3, 1985, called the "Lang Law," the right of the interpreter, like that of record producers, is only a "subsidiary right" of the author's right.

30. See the ruling of March 13, 1957: "Recording and sonorous reproduction of musical pieces and songs constitute an original work protected by the laws of 19–24 July 1793, in that the creation of such a work necessitates for its author a certain technical and professional knowledge, a skill and an ability to implement the best technical procedures in order to ensure a faithful reproduction of music and the recorded voice." Quoted in Marie-Claude Dock, *Étude sur*

le droit d'auteur (Paris: Librairie générale de droit et de jurisprudence, 1963), 168.

31. "Melody is . . . appropriable in itself, whereas harmony and rhythm can be protected only when applied to a melody." Henri Desbois, *Le droit d'auteur en France* (Paris: Dalloz, 1978), 138.

32. Commercial companies that sell sounds are often confronted with legal difficulties: when Bryan Bell, who had worked with the musicians Herbie Hancock and Neil Young, founded a company called Synthbank in order to publish sounds, he found that "the U.S. Copyright Office simply did not provide a means for copyrighting sound apart from music." Steve Jones, "Music and Copyright in the U.S.A.," in *Music and Copyright*, ed. Simon Frith (Edinburgh: Edinburgh University Press, 1993), 73.

33. Quoted in Michael B. Sapherstein, "The Trademark Registrability of the Harley-Davidson Roar" (1998), from Intellectual Property and Technology Forum, Boston College Law School, http://www.bc.edu/bc_org/avp/law/st_org/iptf/articles/index.html.

34. Michel Guerrin, "Les photographes doivent faire face à une avalanche d'autorisations pour photographier un bâtiment, un parc, une gare" ["Photographers Must Face an Avalanche of Authorizations To Photograph a Building, a Park, a Train Station"], *Le Monde*, September 12–13, 1999, 8. In another register, the Caddie company recently sued some newspapers for using its name to describe supermarket shopping carts (see Philippe Rivière, "Mots interdits," *Le monde diplomatique*, January 2000, 7). And a court had already passed a ruling, in 1980, declaring that "the act of using the word BIC, in order to designate a ballpoint pen in a novel, was . . . incorrect and detrimental since it participates in the process of generalizing the brand." Quoted in Lionel Bochurberg, *Le droit de citation* (Paris: Masson, 1994), 5.

35. Cartier-Bresson, "Le honte me monte à la gorge. . ." ["Shame Wells Up in Me. . ."], *Le Monde*, September 12–13, 1999.

36. Quoted (along with the statements that follow) in David Gans, "The Man Who Stole Michael Jackson's Face," *Wired*, February 1995.

37. The Canadian journal *Musicworks* included with its issue no. 47 a cassette of the sonorous plunderings taken from this CD, which no longer exists.

38. As Jacques Derrida writes in *Signéponge* (Paris: Seuil, 1988), 47, a musician cannot "inscribe his signature . . . onto the work: the musician cannot sign in text. He lacks the space to do so, and the spacing of a language (unless he overcodes his music with another semiotic system, musical notation for example)."

39. Quoted in Bochurberg, *Le droit de citation*, 155.

Chapter 4: Listening (to Listening): The Making of the Modern Ear

1. Adorno, *Introduction to the Sociology of Music*, trans. E. B. Ashton (New York: Continuum, 1989).

2. In this order: the "culture consumer" (6), the "emotional listener" (8), the "resentment listener" (10), and, finally, the sixth and seventh types embodying the degree zero of listening, the "listener to whom *music is entertainment*" (16) and the "*indifferent*, the *unmusical*, and the *anti-musical*" listener (17). To be fair to Adorno, we should recall that his typology is obviously not prescriptive: "My point is [not] to disparage representatives of the described listening types negatively," he writes, before adding that it would be "grotesque" to "posture mentally as if mankind existed for the sake of good listening" (18). However, despite all these precautions, Adorno's typology does seem to be *normative*.

3. Noiray, in *L'Avant-scène opera* 172 (July–August 1996): 115.

4. *Stare* ("to stay" in Italian) is often translated "to be," "to be in the process of": *stai ascoltando* for "you are in the process of listening." [In French, "je suis" can mean either "I am" or "I follow."]

5. *Memoirs of Hector Berlioz*, trans. Ernest Newman (New York: Dover, 1960), 53ff.

6. Michael Walter, "Social History of Opera," 332.

7. We can date its French beginnings from the foundation of *Concerts spirituels* in 1725, followed by Gossec's *Concert des Amateurs* in 1769. See James H. Johnson, *Listening in Paris: A Cultural History* (Berkeley and Los Angeles: University of California Press, 1995), 71ff.

8. This systematic conjunction appears clearly in the notes added to Robert's discourse in chapter 15. Note 61 is dedicated to arrangers; here we can find the play on words that Berlioz (as well as Liszt) would adopt a few years later (*arrangements-derangements*): "A profession that is very fashionable today and quite lucrative for the one

who practices it. They began by rising up against the *right* that so-called men of letters assume, to *arrange* in their own way works in the *public domain*; but they ended up regarding this kind of *literary piracy* as a completely natural thing, forgetting that, in a little while, we will have as many versions of one play or one book as there will be *arrangers* or *abbreviators*. . . . Everything is arbitrary in these kinds of *arrangements* or rather *derangements*; the poor authors are tortured without respite, and nothing suggests there will ever be an end to this literary and dramatic inquisition" (331–32). We also find this joint denunciation of arrangement and of the absence of a legislation that is more protective for authors in the remarks devoted to Castil-Blaze: "M. Castil Blaze is the author of a dozen operas for which he has written neither the words, nor the music" (137).

9. Tia DeNora, *Beethoven et la construction du génie* (Paris: Fayard, 1998), 43.

10. Quoted in K. M. Knittel, "Wagner, Deafness, and the Reception of Beethoven's Late Style," *Journal of the American Musicological Society* 51, no. 1 (1998): 53.

11. Quoted in Knittel, ibid., p. 52.

12. Richard Wagner, *Beethoven*, trans. Albert R. Parsons (New York: G. Schirmer, 1883), 63ff.

13. Wagner, in fact, often quotes—in his *Beethoven* as well as in his other writings—Schopenhauer's *The World as Will and Representation*. But, when he speaks of dream, it seems that he relies on the "Essay on Visions" (*Versuch über Geistersehen*), collected in the *Parerga et paralipomena* (1851) of the philosopher, in which Schopenhauer names a certain "organ of dream." Having established, with or following Schopenhauer, that "musical conception . . . can have its origin in that side of consciousness alone which Schopenhauer designates as introverted" (22), Wagner proposes to go "farther . . . in this path" by following Schopenhauer's "profound hypothesis" concerning the phenomenon of "clairvoyance" [*Hellsehen*], as well as his "theory of dreams" (22). It is in fact when "introverted consciousness attains to actual clairvoyance" [*Hellsichtigkeit*] that "*tone* forces its way out" (22). This inner clairvoyance of consciousness is the result, Wagner says, of a "function of the brain . . . which Schopenhauer here terms the organ of dreams" (23). And from then on "the world of sound . . . bears the same relation to the world of

light [i.e., appearances] that the dreaming state does to the waking" (23).

14. In *Three Wagner Essays*, trans. Robert L. Jacobs (London: Eulenburg Books, 1979).

15. Letter from 1930, cited in Josef Rufer, *Das Werk Arnold Schönbergs* (Kassel: Bärenreiter, 1959). I give a translation of this in *Arrangements-dérangements*.

16. Letter dated March 18, 1939, in Arnold Schoenberg, *Correspondance, 1910–1951*, ed. Erwin Stein, trans. Dennis Collins (Paris: Editions Jean-Claude Lattès, 1983), 210.

17. Letter dated March 23, 1918, ibid., 48–49.

18. In this same letter, Schoenberg writes, "I still have the same opinion about cuts that I did before. I am against the removal of tonsils, although I know one can continue to live after a fashion without arms, legs, noses, eyes, tongue, ears, etc." On Schoenbergian organicism and the notion of the "member," see my "Bref Schoenberg," in *La liaison*.

Epilogue: Plastic Listening

1. Michel Butor, *Dialogue avec 33 variations de Ludwig van Beethoven sur une valse de Diabelli* (Paris: Gallimard, 1971).

2. See Carl Dahlhaus, "Thesen über Programmusik," in *Klassische und romantische Musikästhetik* (Laaber, Germany: Laaber-Verlag, 1988), 365ff.

3. Roland Barthes, "Musica Practica," in *Image–Music–Text*, trans. Stephen Heath (New York: Hill and Wang, 1977), 153.

4. One testimonial among others—that of Christian Marclay: "[My] disks were 'prepared' with inscriptions, indications of speed, self-sticking labels to indicate the beginning of an extract or to force the needle to jump and repeat the same phrase in a loop. . . . The score was thus written directly onto the disk." "Le son en images," in *L'Écoute* (Paris: Ircam–L'Harmattan, 2000).

5. Adorno, "The Form of the Phonograph Record," in *Essays on Music*, 277.

6. Adorno, "Worte ohne Lieder," *Vermischte Schriften II* (Frankfurt: Suhrkamp, 1984).

7. See Carl Dahlhaus, *The Idea of Absolute Music*, trans. Roger Lustig (Chicago: University of Chicago Press, 1989), 63: "Literature about music is no mere reflection of what happens in the musical practice of composition, interpretation, and reception, but rather belongs, in a certain sense, to the constituent forces of music itself. For insofar as music does not exhaust itself in the acoustical substrate that underlies it, but only takes shape through categorical ordering of what has been perceived, a change in the system of categories of reception immediately affects the substance of the thing itself."
8. Mauricio Kagel, quoted by Werner Klüppelholz, in *Mauricio Kagel 1970–1980*, (Cologne: DuMont, 1981), 12.
9. Kagel, "Ludwig van," in *Tam-tam* (Paris: Bourgois, 1983).
10. *Duchamp du signe: Ecrits*, ed. Michel Sanouillet (Paris: Flammarion, 1975), 37, 276 (1914 and 1948).